ADVENTURES in LEARNING

Math, language arts, and imagination!

Thinking Kids™
Carson-Dellosa Publishing LLC
Greensboro, North Carolina

Thinking Kids™
Carson-Dellosa Publishing LLC
P.O. Box 35665
Greensboro, NC 27425 USA

Printed in the USA • All rights reserved.   ISBN 978-1-4838-3512-9
01-121177784

TABLE OF CONTENTS

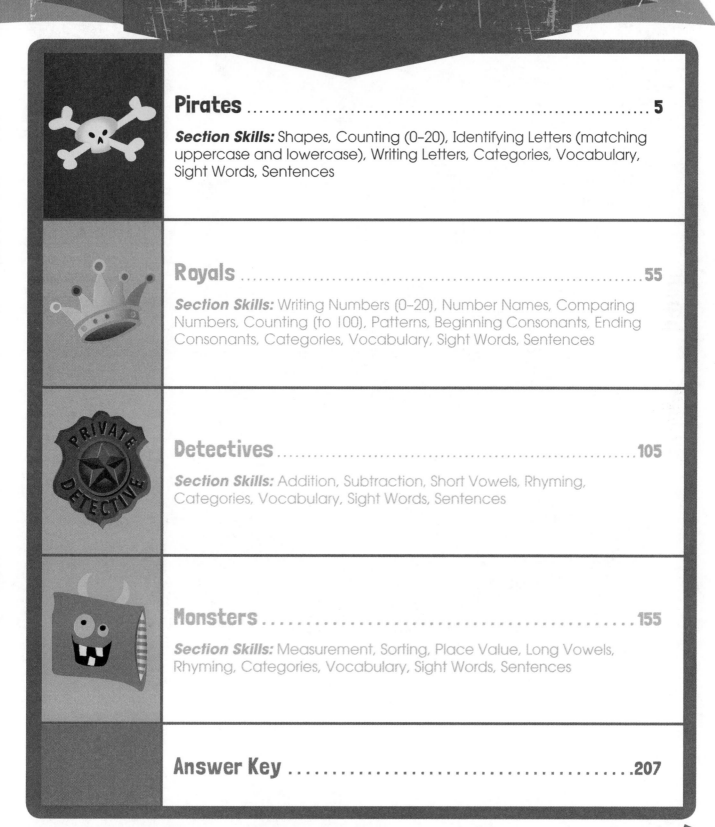

Write the vowel that completes each word.

a e i o u

ch _____ st

sh _____ p

h _____ t

b _____ g

cl _____ ck

fl _____ g

sh _____ ll

f _____ sh

Say the name of each picture.

If it has a long a sound, color it green. If it has a short a sound, color it blue.

Follow the directions.

1. Outline each circle.

2. Color each shape that has 4 sides.

3. Draw a dot in each square.

4. Draw an X on each shape with 3 sides.

Count the shapes in the picture.

Then, write the total number of each shape.

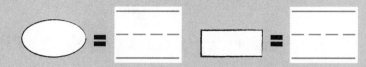

⬭ = _ _ _ _ ▭ = _ _ _ _

◯ = _ _ _ _ ◇ = _ _ _ _

△ = _ _ _ _ ◻ = _ _ _ _

Say the name of each picture.

If it has a **long e** sound, circle it. If it has a **short e** sound, draw a square around it.

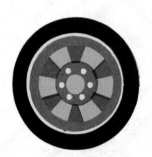

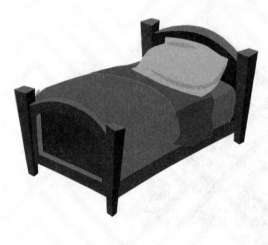

Draw a line from the picture to the word that names it.

Draw a circle around the word if it has the long o sound.

pot

boat

dog

frog

goat

Help Charlie solve each problem.

There are 3 🐬 .

Then, 4 more 🐬 come.

Add to find the sum.

_____

There are 6 🦜 .

two 🦜 fly away.

How many are left?

_____

Charlie has 7 ⚪ .

Izzy has 4 ⚪ .

What is the difference?

_____

I have 8 1¢ .

I get 2 more 1¢ .

What is 8 plus 2?

_____

There are 5 🐟 .

Four 🐟 swim away.

What is 5 minus 4?

_____

There are 4 ⛵ .

Then 4 more ⛵ come.

How many in all?

_____

Help Izzy find the jewels.

Say the name of the picture on each chest. If it has the long i sound, the chest holds jewels. If it has the short i sound, the chest holds shells. Circle the chests with jewels.

Help Charlie add.

4 + 6 = _____

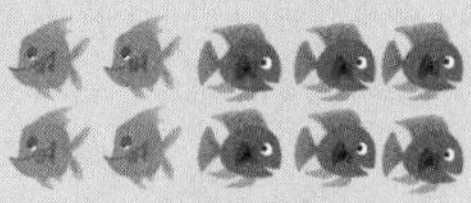

5 + 2 = _____

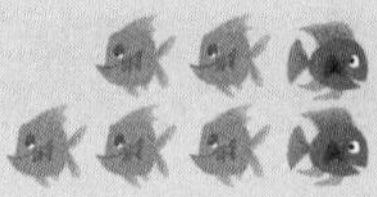

6 + 4 = _____

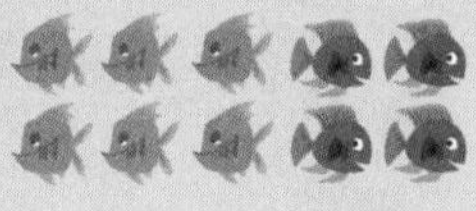

2 + 5 = _____

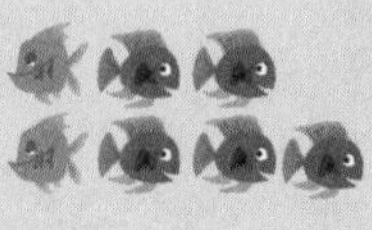

3 + 4 = _____

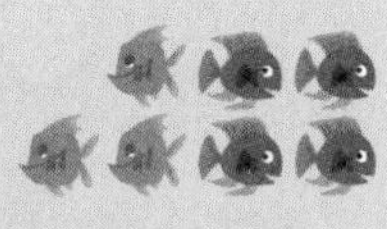

3 + 6 = _____

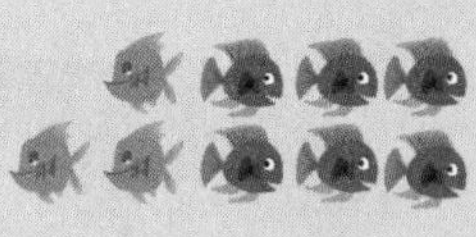

4 + 3 = _____

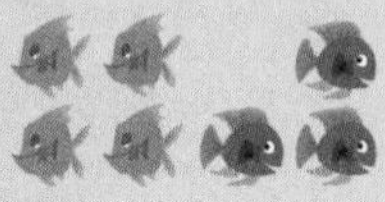

6 + 3 = _____

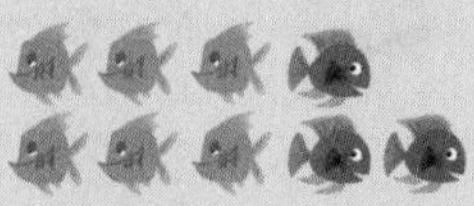

2	5	10	3	7	9
+6	+4	+0	+4	+2	+1

Say the name of each picture.

If it has a **long u** sound, color it red. If it has a short u sound, color it yellow.

Charlie and Izzy need supplies.

The list shows how many of each item they will take. Write the number next to the barrel, and cross out the same number of items. Then subtract to see how many are left. One has been done as an example.

= 7

= 2

= 1

= 3

= 6

= 5

= 8

= 4

Help Izzy sort her books.

Say the name of each book. Listen for the long vowel sound.

Then, draw a line to the correct barrel.

Long **a**   Long **e**   Long **i**   Long **o**   Long **u**

pie   sweet   coat   argue

chain   throw   froze   time

human   clean   play   beach

Subtract to find out how many ships are left.

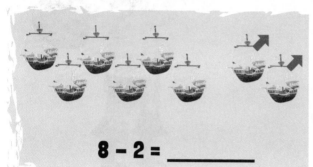

8 − 2 = _____

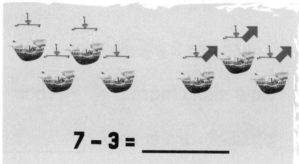

7 − 3 = _____

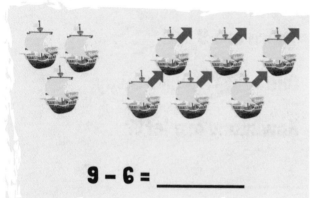

9 − 6 = _____

10 − 7 = _____

6 − 1 = _____

6 − 6 = _____

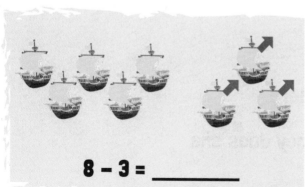

8 − 3 = _____

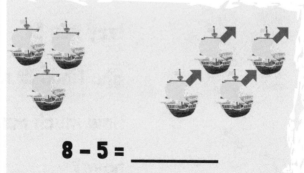

8 − 5 = _____

Help Izzy solve each problem.

There are 8 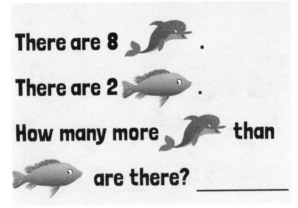 .

There are 2 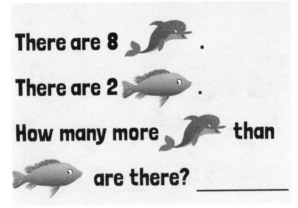 .

How many more 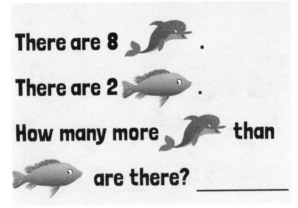 than 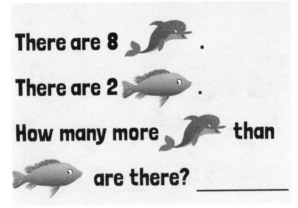 are there? _____

Charlie buys 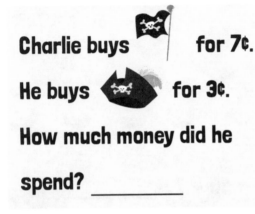 for 7¢.

He buys 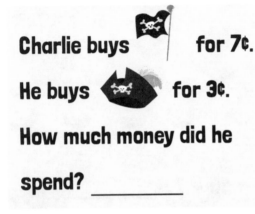 for 3¢.

How much money did he

spend? _____

There are 9 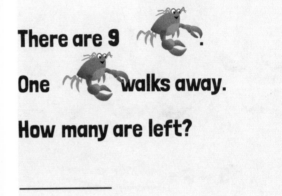 .

One 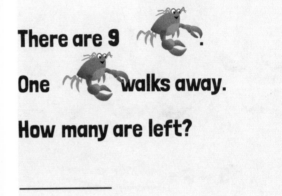 walks away.

How many are left?

_____

An island has 4 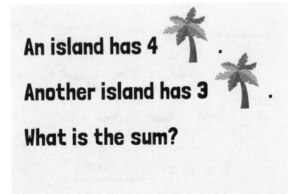 .

Another island has 3 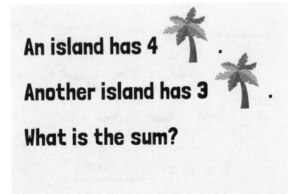 .

What is the sum?

_____

Charlie has 10¢.

He buys for 8¢.

How much money does he

have left? _____

Izzy has 5¢.

She finds 3¢ more.

How much money does she

have? _____

Say the name of each picture.
On each line, write the vowel that completes the word.
Color the short vowel pictures. Circle the long vowel pictures.

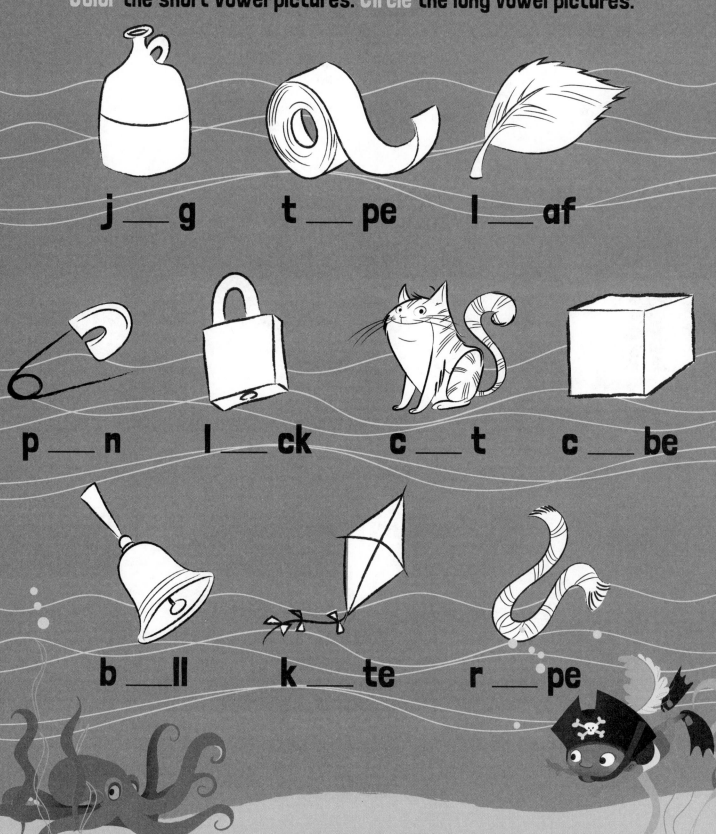

j __ g   t __ pe   l __ af

p __ n   l __ ck   c __ t   c __ be

b __ ll   k __ te   r __ pe

Choose the vowel team to complete each word. Fill in the blanks.

 s ___ ___ l

ai   ee   ay

 b ___ ___ t

oo   ow   oa

 b ___ ___ ts

oo   ow   oa

 p ___ ___ s

ay   ea   ee

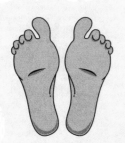 f ___ ___ t

ea   ee   ai

 h ___ ___

ai   ay   oa

 sp ___ ___ n

ea   oa   oo

 sn ___ ___

ow   oo   oa

A noun is a word that names a person, place, or thing.

Cut out the nouns below. Then, sort them into the correct boxes.

Person    **Place**    **Thing**

ship	apple	zoo	store
child	ocean	baby	pirate
tree	table	map	sailor

Add or subtract.

$$2 \atop +4$$ $$4 \atop +2$$ $$6 \atop -2$$ $$6 \atop -4$$

$$1 \atop +1$$ $$1 \atop -0$$

2 + 0 = _____

0 + 2 = _____

2 − 0 = _____

2 − 2 = _____

5 + 0 = _____

0 + 5 = _____

5 − 5 = _____

5 − 0 = _____

$$2 \atop +3$$ $$3 \atop +2$$ $$5 \atop -2$$ $$5 \atop -3$$

$$6 \atop +0$$ $$0 \atop +6$$ $$6 \atop -0$$ $$6 \atop -6$$

A blend is made by combining two consonant sounds (Example: floor).

The name of each picture below begins with a blend. Circle the beginning blend for each picture.

bl
fl
cl

cl
fl
gl

fl
cl
gl

dr
br
tr

dr
tr
br

tr
dr
br

Charlie and Izzy are having a beach party!
Say the names of things in the picture.
Circle words that begin with s blends: sl, sm, sn, sp, st.

Count the coins.

Write the number of tens and ones. Then, write the total. In the last box, draw coins to show the tens and ones. Write the total.

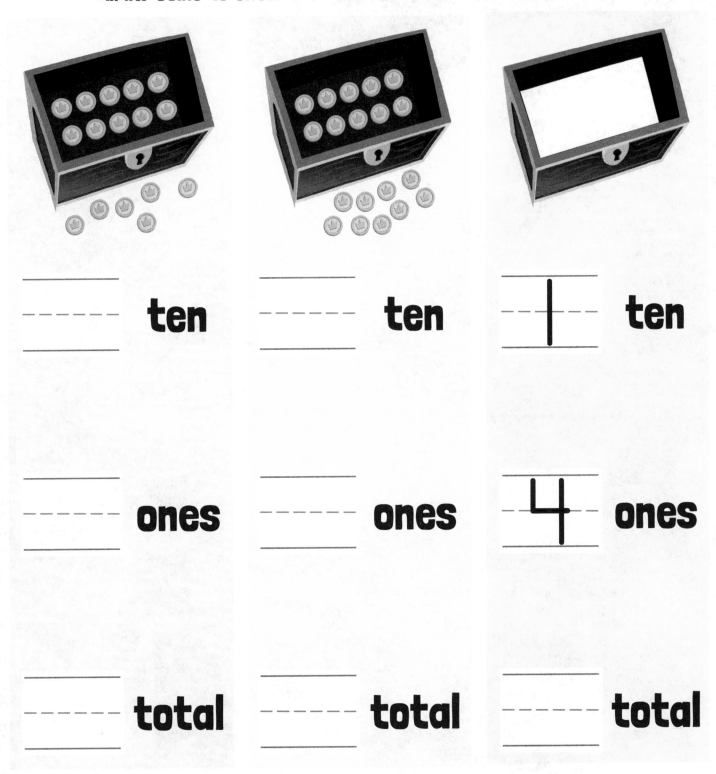

Count the jewels.

Write the number of tens and ones. Then, write the total. In the last box, draw jewels to show the tens and ones. Write the total.

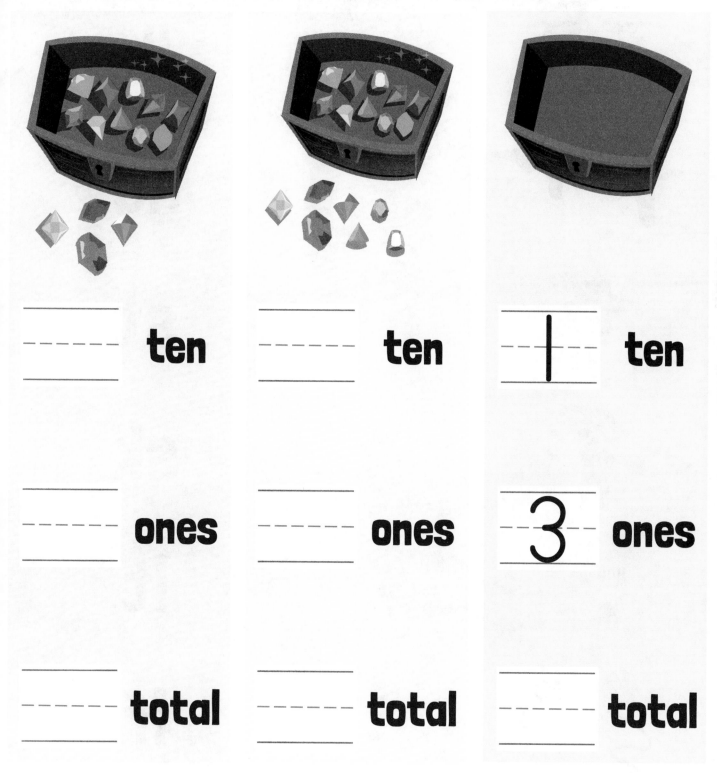

----------- ten

----------- ones

----------- total

----------- ten

----------- ones

----------- total

-----1----- ten

-----3----- ones

----------- total

Draw a line from the picture to the blend that ends the word.

lk

nd

st

sk

lt

lf

A digraph is a pair of letters that make one sound together.

Name each picture. Listen for the digraphs ch, sh, and th. If the name begins with a diagraph, circle the picture. If the name ends with a diagraph, underline the picture.

Help Charlie catch the stowaways!

Cross out the word on each ship that does not belong.

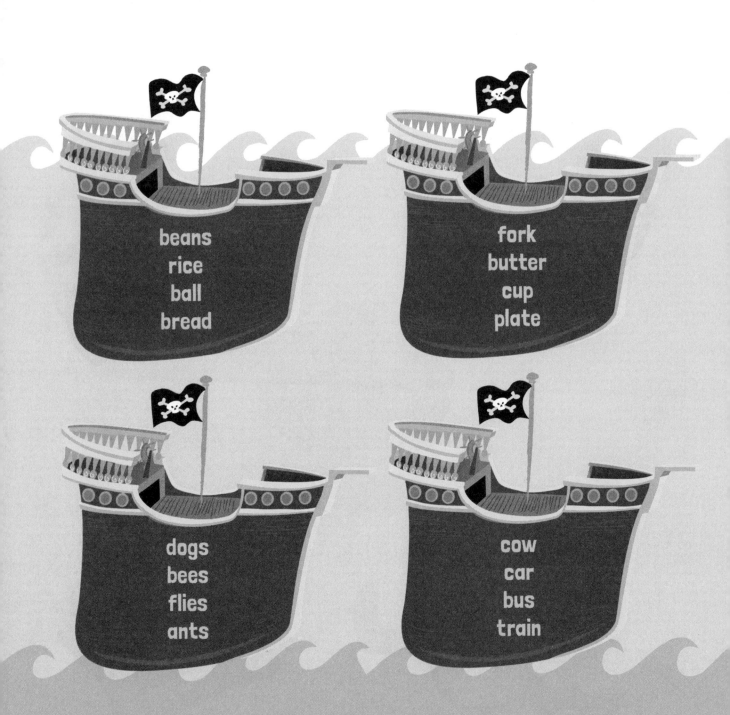

beans
rice
ball
bread

fork
butter
cup
plate

dogs
bees
flies
ants

cow
car
bus
train

13

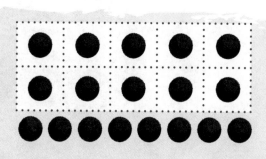

_____

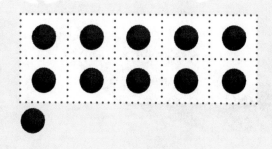

_____

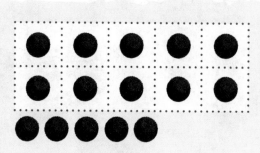

_____

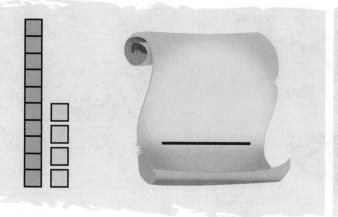

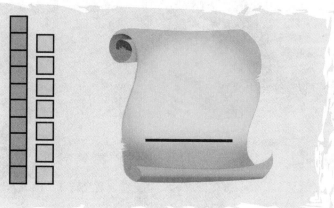

Number the boats as follows: 1 - long, 2 - medium, 3 - short.

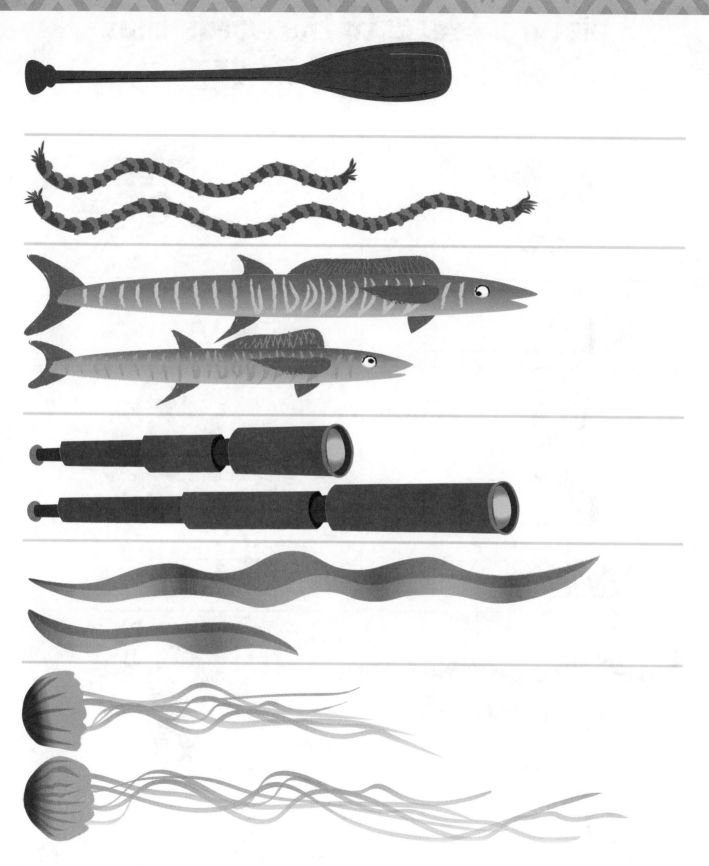

The digraph ng makes the ending sound in words like ring. Say the name of each picture. Add ng to the words that end with the sound of ng.

ki

sw

wi

fi

lo

si

Say the name of each picture.

Write the digraph from the box that you hear at the beginning or end of the word.

ch   sh   th   wh   ng

Number the objects as follows:

1 - long, 2 - medium, 3 - short.

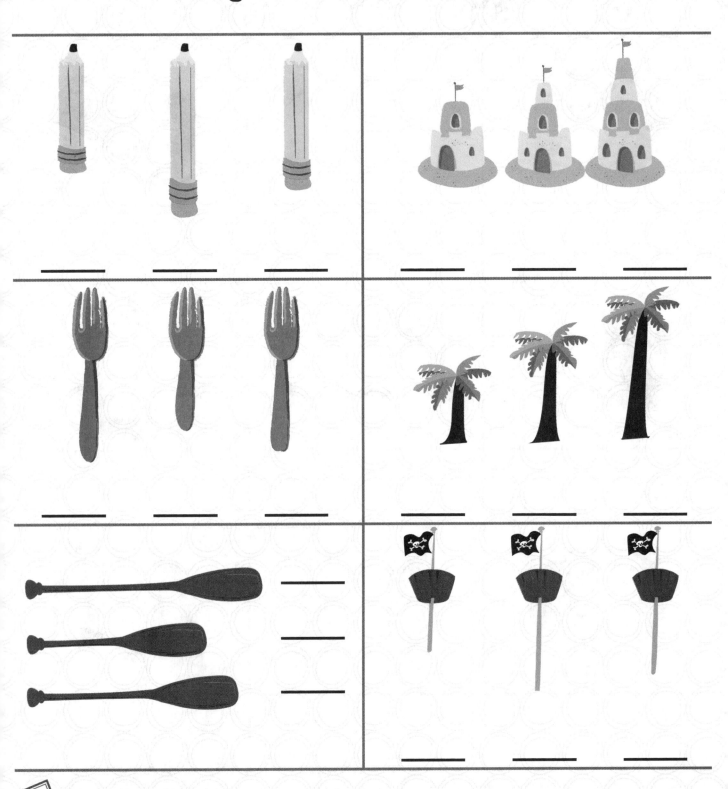

Add or subtract.

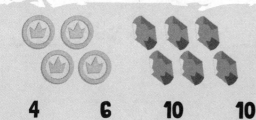

4	6	10	10
+6	+4	−6	−4

4	8
+4	−4

2 + 7 = _____

7 + 2 = _____

9 − 2 = _____

9 − 7 = _____

8 + 2 = _____

2 + 8 = _____

10 − 2 = _____

10 − 8 = _____

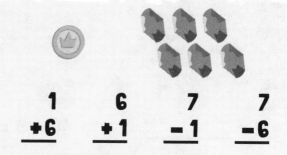

5	3	8	8
+3	+5	−5	−3

1	6	7	7
+6	+1	−1	−6

Help Izzy find the answers to these problems.

1 + 3 = _____   4 − 3 = _____   4 + 5 = _____

6 + 2 = _____   7 − 2 = _____   8 − 5 = _____

9 − 4 = _____   10 − 5 = _____

4 + 3 = _____

6 + 3 = _____

8 + 2 = _____   10 − 3 = _____

Help Charlie organize the hold.
Circle the object on each shelf that does not belong.

Write words from the box on the flags that describe them.

Izzy   four   Max   cat   dog   yellow
blue   red   pig   Charlie   two   one

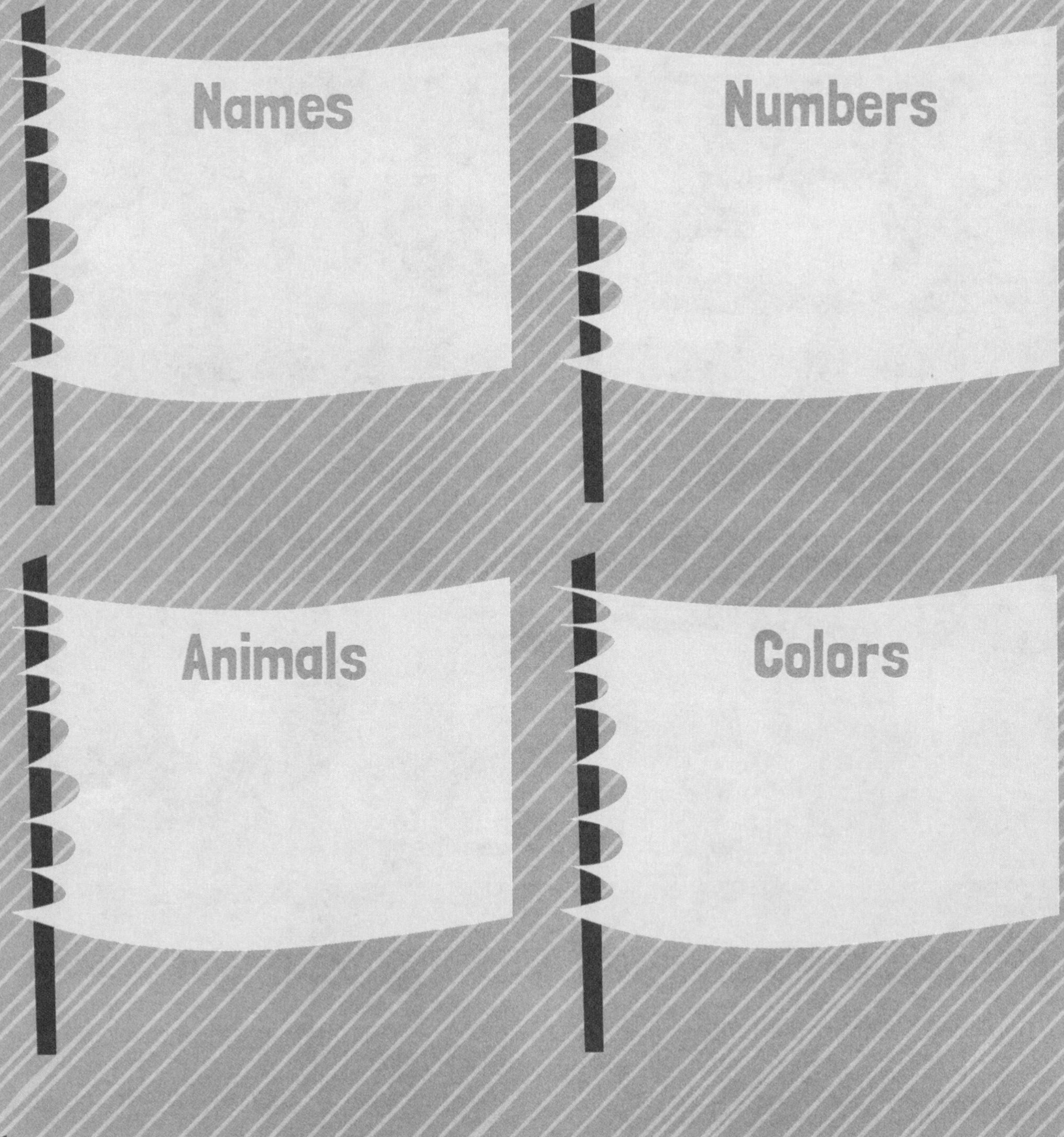

Names

Numbers

Animals

Colors

Draw shapes to fit each rule.

Four Equal Sides

Three Corners

No Corners

Four Corners
Two Pairs of Equal Sides

Help Izzy find the answers to these problems.

7 + 3 = _____   5 - 2 = _____   3 + 6 = _____

2 + 7 = _____   6 - 3 = _____   9 - 5 = _____

4 - 4 = _____   10 - 7 = _____   3 + 2 = _____

4 + 2 = _____

10 - 4 = _____

8 - 7 = _____

Circle the word in each row that is most like the first word in the row.

bee   fish   ant   snake

grin   smile   frown   mad

bag   jar   sack   box

bird   dog   cat   duck

ship   boat   bike   car

round   square   ball   star

Help Izzy build a castle!

First, circle the correct name of each shape below.
Then, use the shapes to make a castle on the next page.
Use each shape as often as you need.

triangle

circle

rectangle

square

rectangle

circle

square

triangle

rectangle

triangle

square

circle

Read each sentence and look at the underlined word.

Circle the word that means almost the same thing.

Charlie is a <u>nice</u> pirate.	mad kind bad
The bird is in the <u>tall</u> tree.	green pretty big
Izzy is <u>tired</u>.	sleepy sad little
The <u>little</u> fish swam.	tall funny small
The <u>quick</u> crab ran.	slow mean fast
The <u>happy</u> girl smiled.	glad sad good

When you read a sentence, a noun is what the sentence is about.

Complete each sentence below with a noun.

The _____ is tiny.

small   fish   swim

The _____ is green.

funny   stop   bird

The _____ is sailing.

float   ship   big

The _____ is hot.

sun   shine   yellow

An s at the end of a noun usually means it is plural, or shows more than one.

Look at each group. Circle the correct word.

dolphin   dolphins

pail   pails

shell   shells

chest   chests

tree   trees

Help Izzy count to 20.
Write the number that is hidden under each object.

1   **2**   **3**   **4**   **5**

6   **7**      **9**   **10**

   12   **13**   **15**

16      **18**      **20**

 = _ _ _ _ _ _ _ _ _ _ _ _

 = _ _ _ _ _ _ _ _ _ _ _ _

 = _ _ _ _ _ _ _ _ _ _ _ _

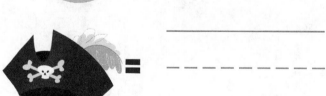 = _ _ _ _ _ _ _ _ _ _ _ _

⚓ = _ _ _ _ _ _ _ _ _ _ _

Draw a line from each boat to the noun that names its cargo.

balls   **flags**   **cat**   **stars**

Pay close attention to whether the word ends in s.

cats   ball   star   flag

Color the 6 fish. From smallest to biggest, use these colors: green, red, blue, orange, yellow, purple.

Charlie and Izzy are counting their jewels, but they missed 6 numbers.

Write the missing numbers.

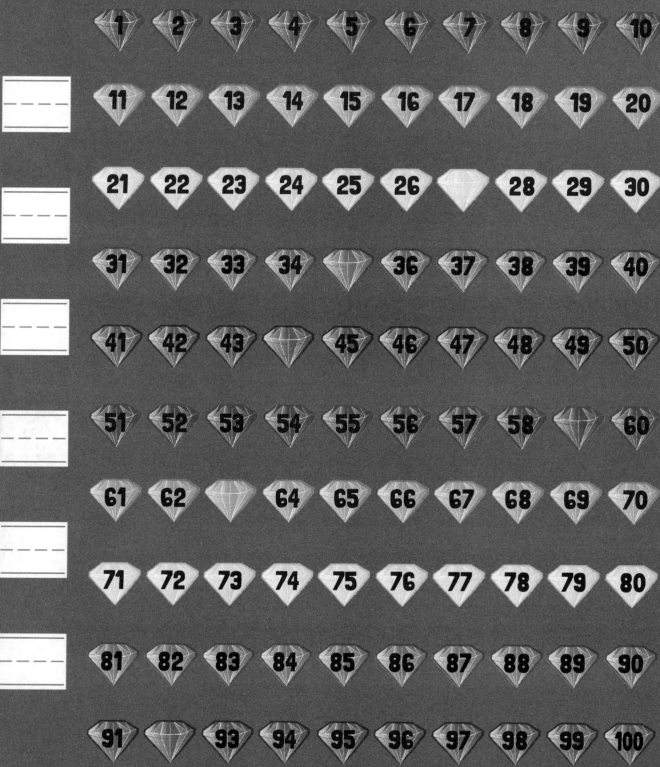

1 2 3 4 5 6 7 8 9 10

_ _ _   11 12 13 14 15 16 17 18 19 20

_ _ _   21 22 23 24 25 26 ___ 28 29 30

   31 32 33 34 ___ 36 37 38 39 40

_ _ _   41 42 43 ___ 45 46 47 48 49 50

_ _ _   51 52 53 54 55 56 57 58 ___ 60

   61 62 ___ 64 65 66 67 68 69 70

_ _ _   71 72 73 74 75 76 77 78 79 80

_ _ _   81 82 83 84 85 86 87 88 89 90

   91 ___ 93 94 95 96 97 98 99 100

Proper nouns are names of particular people, places, things, or events. Proper nouns always begin with a capital letter.

Underline the proper noun in each sentence.

Please tell Izzy to walk the dog.

Let's bake a cake for Charlie.

His birthday is in May.

The dragon's name is Daisy.

The castle is near the town of Royalton.

What will you wear for Halloween?

Write Charlie's name and Izzy's name. Then write your first and last name. Remember: names are proper nouns. Draw a picture of yourself in the box.

Help Izzy sort the animals into categories.

Cut out each animal name. Glue or tape it into the correct box.

Pet	Zoo	Pretend

unicorn	hippo	dragon	tiger
beagle	hamster	elephant	canary
troll	otter	rabbit	Bigfoot

Help Izzy use the number line to add!
Count on to solve each problem.

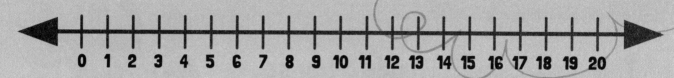

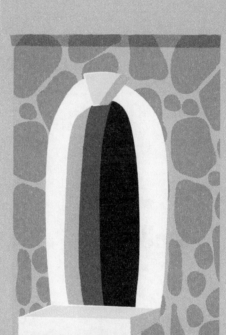

10	12	11	11	14	15
+ 8	+ 5	+ 7	+ 3	+ 2	+ 4

Write a noun from the box to tell who is doing something in each sentence.

The _____ rode a horse.

boy   man   woman

The _____ drank tea.

girls   children   men

The _____ smiled.

mother   girl   women

The _____ washed the happy dog.

woman   children   man

Some _____ like to bake.

fathers   person   people

Help Charlie use the number line to subtract!
Count back to solve each problem.

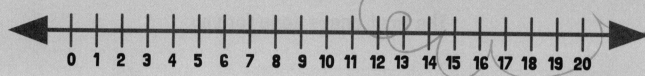

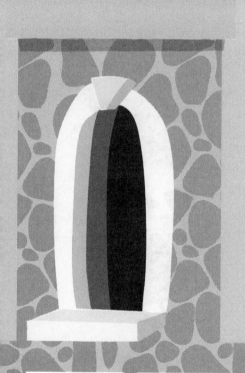

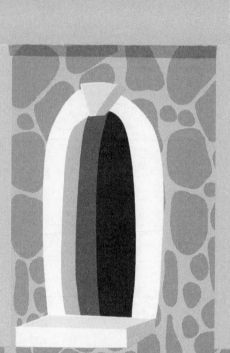

20	19	16	13	16	14
− 8	− 5	− 3	− 7	− 8	−12

Add 's to each proper or common noun to make it possessive.

Then, write the word for each picture to show what is owned.
The first one is done for you.

Izzy **'s** **jewel**

Charlie ____ ____

The bird ____ ____

The cat ____ ____

The dragon ____ ____

Help Charlie and Izzy count forward and backward. Write the missing numbers.

25, 26, _____, 28, 29, _____, 31, _____, 33, _____

48, _____, 50, 51, 52, _____, 54, _____, _____, 57

_____, 71, 72, 73, _____, _____, 76, _____, 78, 79

84, 85, 86, _____, 88, _____, 90, _____, 92, _____

32, 31, 30, _____, 28, 27, _____, _____, 24, _____

_____, 49, 48, 47, _____, 45, _____, 43, _____, 41

65, _____, 63, 62, _____, 60, _____, 58, 57, _____

81, _____, 79, _____, 77, 76, 75, _____, _____, 72

Charlie and Izzy are in the royal library. Some of the books are on the wrong shelves. Read the titles on each shelf. Circle the book with the word that does not belong.

Trains   Jets   Planes   Hands   Cars

Rose   Tulip   Trees   Daisy   Sunflower

Lake   Ocean   Chair   Pond   River

Help Charlie solve the problems.

There are 10 .

There are 2 .

How many and

total? _____

There are 8 .

There are 6 .

How many crowns in all?

_____

There are 5 .

There are 7 .

How many dresses in all?

_____

Izzy puts 11 on the table.

Then she adds 3 more

How many in all?

_____

There are 9 .

There are 4 .

Find the total number of birds.

_____

There are 9 .

There are 4 .

Find the total.

_____

Pronouns can be used in place of some nouns.

Write the pronoun He, She, or They in each sentence below.

Charlie likes cookies.

_____ likes cookies.

Izzy drinks tea.

_____ drinks tea.

Charlie and Izzy have good manners.

_____ have good manners.

Help Izzy find the secret path across the moat.

Look at each subtraction problem. The stones with wrong answers will sink!
Find the path with correct answers.

$$\begin{array}{r} 20 \\ -\ 3 \\ \hline 17 \end{array}$$
$$\begin{array}{r} 19 \\ -\ 5 \\ \hline 12 \end{array}$$
$$\begin{array}{r} 20 \\ -\ 9 \\ \hline 10 \end{array}$$
$$\begin{array}{r} 14 \\ -\ 7 \\ \hline 8 \end{array}$$

$$\begin{array}{r} 15 \\ -\ 8 \\ \hline 7 \end{array}$$
$$\begin{array}{r} 16 \\ -\ 5 \\ \hline 11 \end{array}$$
$$\begin{array}{r} 17 \\ -\ 7 \\ \hline 8 \end{array}$$
$$\begin{array}{r} 12 \\ -\ 5 \\ \hline 6 \end{array}$$

$$\begin{array}{r} 19 \\ -\ 2 \\ \hline 15 \end{array}$$
$$\begin{array}{r} 12 \\ -\ 9 \\ \hline 3 \end{array}$$
$$\begin{array}{r} 17 \\ -\ 5 \\ \hline 12 \end{array}$$
$$\begin{array}{r} 13 \\ -\ 4 \\ \hline 5 \end{array}$$

$$\begin{array}{r} 20 \\ -\ 8 \\ \hline 14 \end{array}$$
$$\begin{array}{r} 13 \\ -\ 6 \\ \hline 6 \end{array}$$
$$\begin{array}{r} 11 \\ -\ 2 \\ \hline 9 \end{array}$$
$$\begin{array}{r} 10 \\ -\ 8 \\ \hline 18 \end{array}$$

Help Charlie find the answers to these problems.

$$\begin{array}{r} 9 \\ +\ 5 \\ \hline \end{array}$$ $$\begin{array}{r} 11 \\ -\ 6 \\ \hline \end{array}$$ $$\begin{array}{r} 12 \\ +\ 7 \\ \hline \end{array}$$

$$\begin{array}{r} 12 \\ +\ 3 \\ \hline \end{array}$$ $$\begin{array}{r} 16 \\ -\ 6 \\ \hline \end{array}$$ $$\begin{array}{r} 9 \\ +\ 7 \\ \hline \end{array}$$

$$\begin{array}{r} 15 \\ -\ 4 \\ \hline \end{array}$$ $$\begin{array}{r} 18 \\ -\ 7 \\ \hline \end{array}$$

$$\begin{array}{r} 13 \\ +\ 3 \\ \hline \end{array}$$ $$\begin{array}{r} 14 \\ +\ 2 \\ \hline \end{array}$$

$$\begin{array}{r} 10 \\ -\ 9 \\ \hline \end{array}$$ $$\begin{array}{r} 11 \\ +\ 4 \\ \hline \end{array}$$

Possessive pronouns tell who owns something.

Write a possessive pronoun from the box to replace each word in bold type.

her	my	his	their	its

Charlie's birthday = _____ birthday

Charlie's and Izzy's jewels = _____ jewels

the **horse's** tail = _____ tail

the book **belonging to me** = _____ book

Izzy's throne = _____ throne

Each goblet has 10 jewels. Count the tens.

Then, write the total number of jewels.

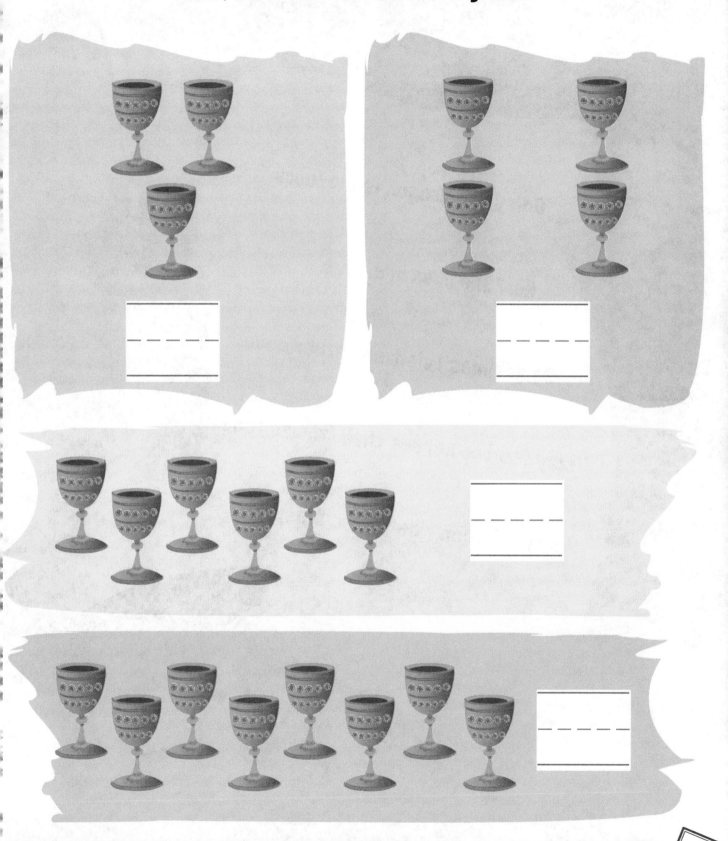

Help Charlie choose the right pronouns.

Circle the pronoun that correctly completes
each sentence.

Daisy the dragon is our/ours friend.

Her/She lives in a cave.

Sometimes I visit she's/her cave.

Izzy fed the horses their/theirs food.

Now we/is can ride to see Daisy!

Each goblet has 10 jewels. Draw goblets to show each number.

The first one has been done for you.

50	**20**
10	**30**

Finish the fact family portraits.

The numbers to use are shown at the bottom of each frame.
The first one has been done for you.

$$7 + 5 = 12$$
$$5 + 7 = 12$$
$$12 - 7 = 5$$
$$12 - 5 = 7$$

5, 7, 12

___ + ___ = ___

___ + ___ = ___

___ − ___ = ___

___ − ___ = ___

4, 6, 10

___ + ___ = ___

___ + ___ = ___

___ − ___ = ___

___ − ___ = ___

5, 6, 11

___ + ___ = ___

___ + ___ = ___

___ − ___ = ___

___ − ___ = ___

6, 7, 13

Addition, Subtraction

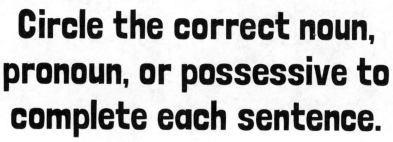

Circle the correct noun, pronoun, or possessive to complete each sentence.

Have you seen Izzies/Izzy's crown?

Charlie wants to visit London/london someday.

Daisy sleeps in hers/her cave at night.

Twelve flag/flags fly above the castle.

On Monday, three childs/children will come for tea.

They/Them will bring cupcakes.

Finish the fact family portraits.

The numbers to use are shown at the bottom of each frame.

____ + ____ = ____

____ + ____ = ____

____ − ____ = ____

____ − ____ = ____

4, 8, 12

____ + ____ = ____

____ + ____ = ____

____ − ____ = ____

____ − ____ = ____

2, 9, 11

____ + ____ = ____

____ + ____ = ____

____ − ____ = ____

____ − ____ = ____

3, 10, 13

____ + ____ = ____

____ + ____ = ____

____ − ____ = ____

____ − ____ = ____

5, 9, 14

Circle the correctly spelled word in each set. Then, write it on the lines.

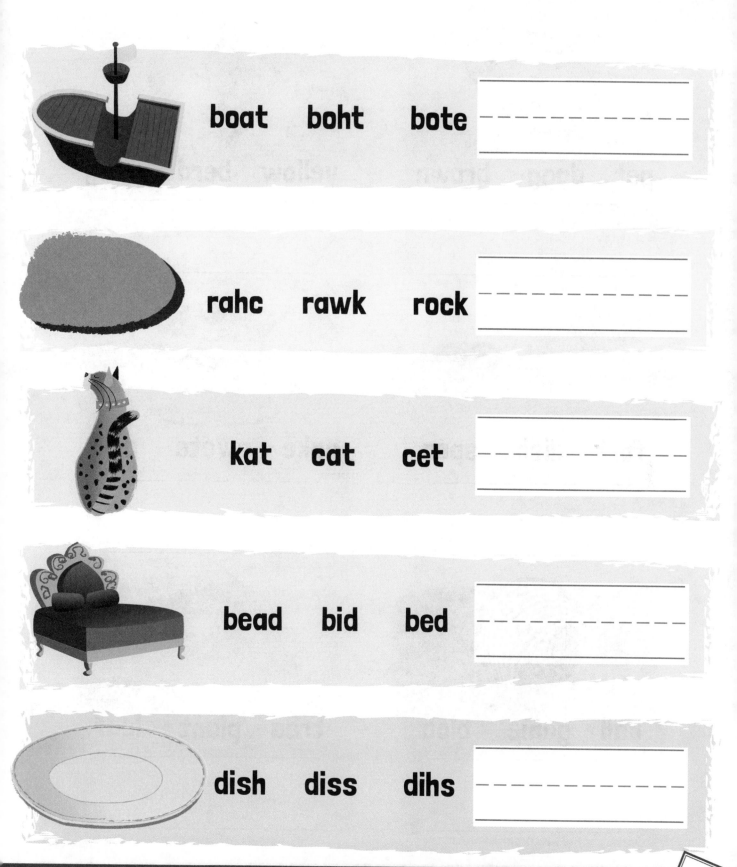

boat   boht   bote

rahc   rawk   rock

kat   cat   cet

bead   bid   bed

dish   diss   dihs

Circle the misspelled word in each set. Then, write the correct spelling on the line.

pet   dogg   brown

yellow   berd   wing

fork   dish   spon

cake   swete   pink

ball   game   bloo

trea   plant   leaf

Read each sentence. Draw a picture to show how Izzy or Charlie feels.

Izzy was happy when the rain stopped.

Izzy was thrilled when the sun came out.

Charlie saw a big spider.

Charlie saw a gigantic spider.

Help Izzy measure. She is using spoons to measure the lengths. Write the measurement on each line.

The dog is about _____ spoons long.

The bird is about _____ spoon long.

Each crown has 10 jewels. Count the groups of crowns, and write the number by the word tens. Count the other jewels, and write the number by the word ones. Then, write the total.

+ = _____ tens + _____ ones = _____

+ = _____ tens + _____ ones = _____

+ = _____ tens + _____ ones = _____

+ = _____ tens + _____ ones = _____

Charlie is unsure what some of these words mean.

Draw a line from each red word to a word on the next page that has a more familiar meaning.

Izzy found a blade of grass.

Daisy is a rare type of dragon.

My horse likes to run over the mounds near the castle.

There is an enormous cloud in the sky.

knife   huge

piece   gray

uncooked   special

sand   scary

wheel   old

small hills

mountains

Circle the shape of the bottom face of each figure.

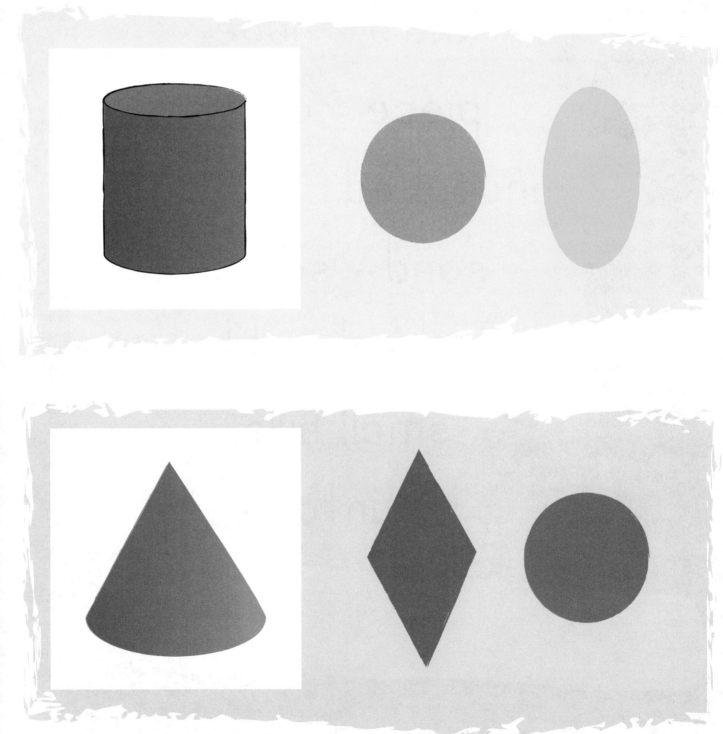

Circle the shape of the bottom face of each figure.

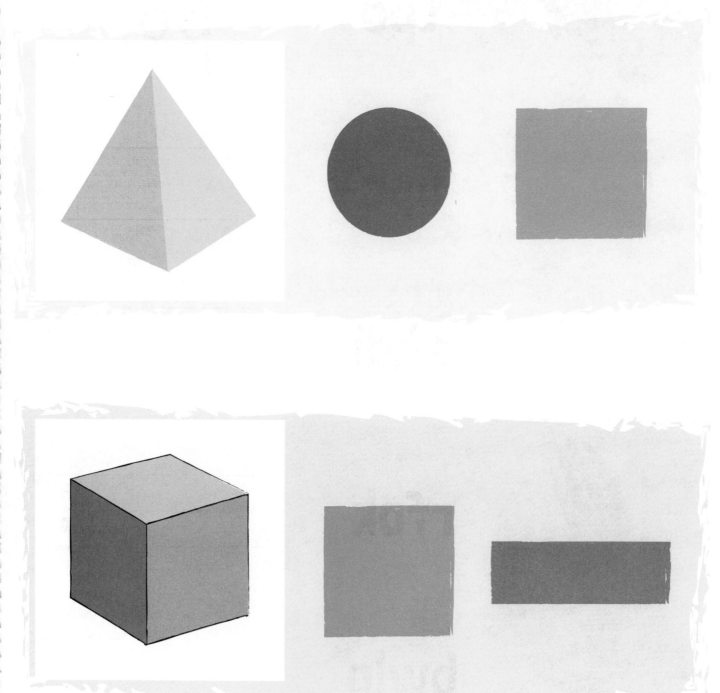

The letters in each word are mixed up.

Write each word correctly. The first one is done for you.

tpo   pot

upc

shdi

rfok

bwlo

Cut out the line of coins.
Use the coins to measure each object.

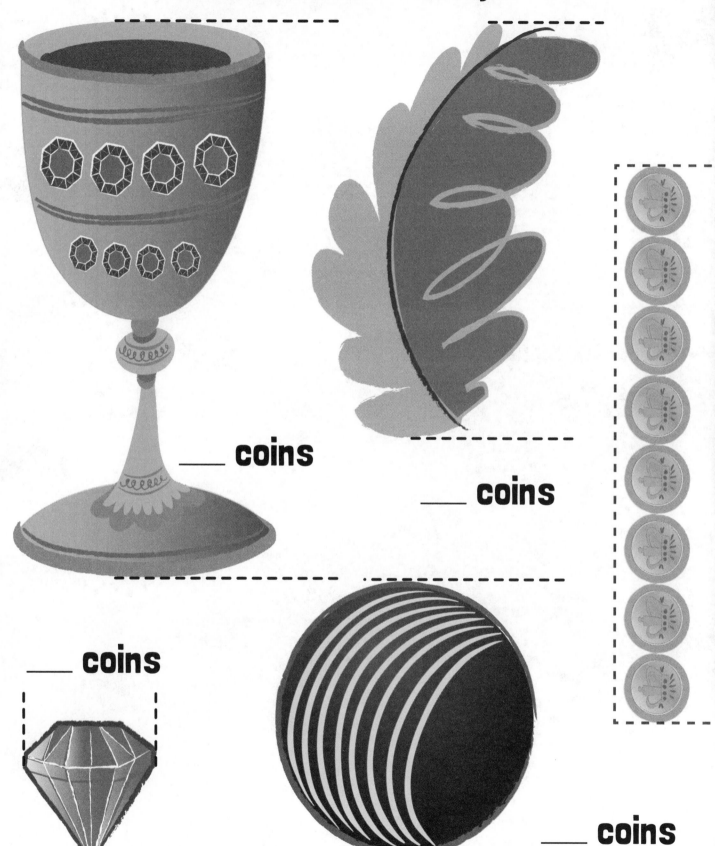

___ coins

___ coins

___ coins

___ coins

Each sentence has one incorrect noun or pronoun. Circle the mistake. Write the correct noun or pronoun on the line.

Charlie ate he's lunch.

_____

Please tell izzy to bring me my crown.

_____

Where is yours goblet?

_____

Ten flag fly above the castle.

_____

The horses mane is very pretty.

_____

Mine jewels are in the safe.

_____

The baker made seven fancy cake.

_____

Help Izzy and Charlie defend the kingdom.

Circle the shield with the number that matches each description.
Then, write the circled numbers from least to greatest.

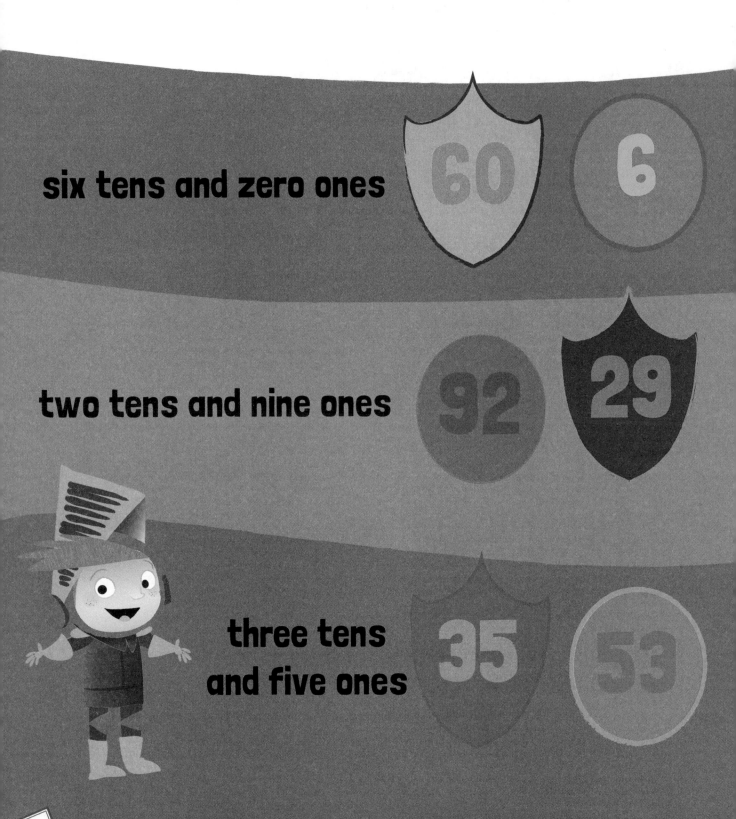

six tens and zero ones

60   6

two tens and nine ones

92   29

three tens
and five ones

35   53

nine tens and two ones 92 29

one ten and seven ones 71 17

eight tens and three ones

38 83

least   greatest

Daisy is a strong dragon. Circle the word in each pair that has the stronger meaning.

hot boiling	slammed closed	exhausted tired
crashed fell	gigantic big	hungry starving
cool icy	upset furious	looked stared
screamed said	damp soaked	pounded tapped

Help Charlie sort the words into categories. Write each word in the box where it belongs.

Food	Clothes	Toys

dress	ball	egg	doll
hat	plum	rice	pants
blocks	sled	shirt	soup

Fill in the missing letters for each word.

_ h _ r t

p _ _ t s

s h _ e _

s o c _ _

_ _ o r t s

_ _ _ e s _

Cut out the line of jewels.
Use the jewels to measure each object.

___ **jewels**

___ **jewels**

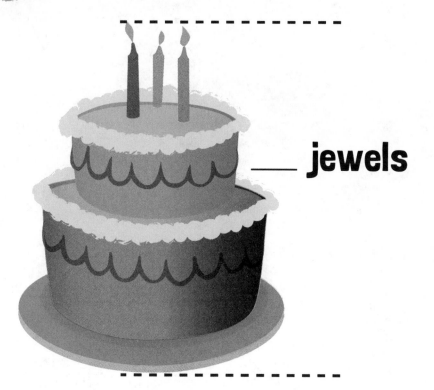

___ **jewels**

___ **jewels**

Write the color word that best describes each picture. Use correct spelling.

tree

door

feather

dog

bird

hat

ball

cloud

Read each sentence. Draw a picture to show how Izzy or Charlie feels.

Izzy was nervous about the spelling test.

Izzy was terrified about the troll at the door.

Charlie walked across the bridge.

Charlie raced across the bridge.

Circle the crowns with words that have **similar** meanings.

Cross out the crowns with words that have **opposite** meanings.

grin/smile

over/above

open/closed

stream/creek

fly/soar

dry/moist

night/evening

broken/whole

front/back

secret/hidden

Write >, <, or = to compare each pair of numbers.

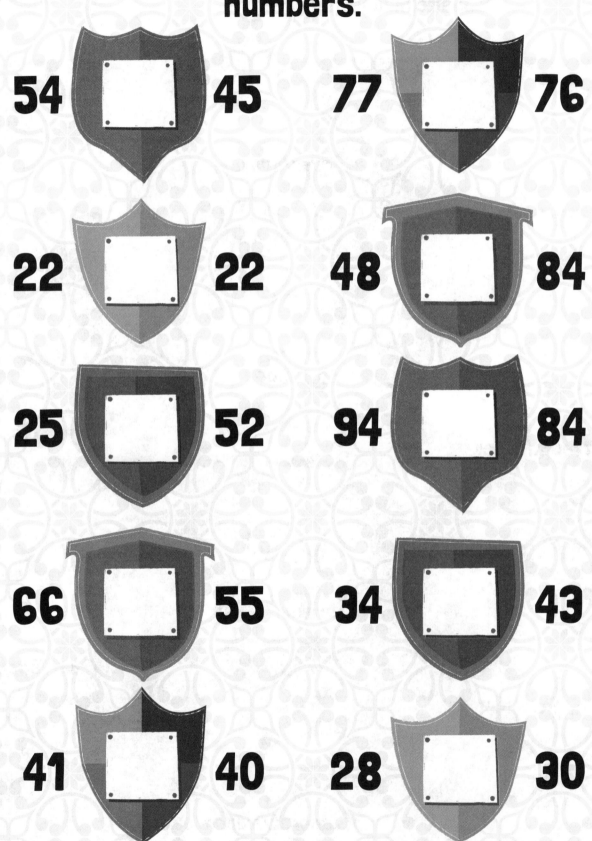

54 [ ] 45

77 [ ] 76

22 [ ] 22

48 [ ] 84

25 [ ] 52

94 [ ] 84

66 [ ] 55

34 [ ] 43

41 [ ] 40

28 [ ] 30

Add or subtract each row. Then, add or subtract each column. Write the answers on the lines.

3	+	5	=	---
+		+		+
6	+	3	=	---
=		=		=
---	+	---	=	---

4	+	7	=	---
+		+		+
3	+	6	=	---
=		=		=
---	+	---	=	---

13	–	8	=	---
–		–		–
5	–	4	=	---
=		=		=
---	–	---	=	---

16	–	7	=	---
–		–		–
9	–	5	=	---
=		=		=
---	–	---	=	---

Use context clues to make the best choice for each blue word's meaning. Circle your choice.

Izzy and Charlie invited all their friends to a huge feast. For dessert, they served 100 different cakes!

a sporting event   a long hike   a big meal

The way Daisy the dragon makes fire is fascinating to watch.

very interesting   very scary   very strange

Izzy tried to calm her horse after it was scared by a snake.

move   quiet   anger

Armor is worn to protect a knight during battle.

keep warm   keep safe   keep hidden

Charlie discovered an old painting in castle's basement.

opened   broke   found

Help Izzy solve the problems. Use the tens and ones blocks to add.

35
+ 8
———

23
+ 5
———

47
+ 2
———

53
+ 6
———

29
+ 3
———

Verbs are words that tell what a person or a thing can do. Draw a line between the verbs below and the pictures that show action.

look

play

brush

read

grow

Look at the picture and read the words.
Write an action word in each sentence below.

fly

talk

drives

runs

Charlie and Izzy _____ about the case.

The robber _____ away.

Birds _____ over the buildings.

A van _____ down the street.

Help Charlie add.

17
+ 2
___

20
+ 5
___

18
+ 4
___

36
+ 3
___

24
+ 7
___

32
+ 7
___

14
+ 8
___

41
+ 6
___

29
+ 8
___

34
+ 6
___

27
+ 4
___

31
+ 9
___

19
+ 4
___

33
+ 9
___

51
+ 4
___

49
+ 7
___

What time is it?

Write the time shown on each clock. One has been done as an example.

___ : ___

5 : 00

___ : ___

___ : ___

___ : ___

___ : ___

Help Izzy and Charlie find the right verb.
Circle the verb that correctly completes the sentence.

The dog bark/barks when it sees a cat.

The plants grow/grows taller when
I water them.

Three balls roll/rolls down the hill.

Charlie look/looks for clues.

Izzy read/reads her notes.

They solve/solves the case.

The children play/plays soccer.

When the subject of a sentence is singular, you use a singular verb. When the subject of a sentence is plural, you use a plural verb. Write a verb from the correct box to complete each sentence.

Singular Verbs
finds
chases
jumps

Plural Verbs
find
chase
jump

Charlie _____ a clue.

Izzy _____ a ball across the playground.

Charlie and Izzy _____ over a puddle.

They _____ a dog around the lake.

Charlie _____ into the pool.

Charlie and Izzy _____ a pretty rock.

Count each set of objects. Write the number word to show how many.

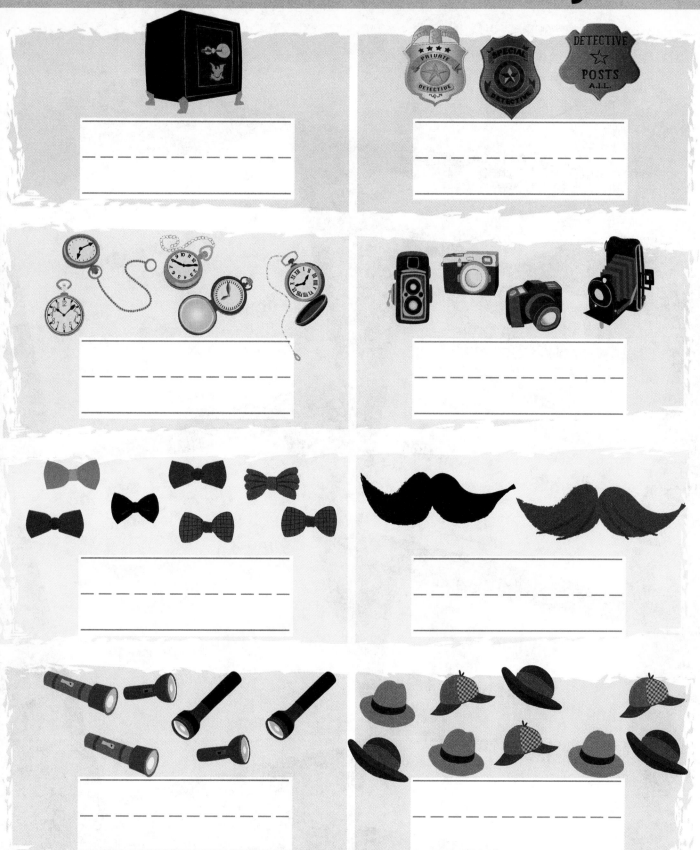

Help Charlie solve these problems.

Charlie has 22 👓 in a box.

He has 9 more 👓 in another box.

How many 👓 in all?

_____

There are 41 ⛺ at Campground One.

There are 5 ⛺ at Campground Two.

How many ⛺ in all?

_____

Izzy saw 35 🔦 at the first store.

She saw 7 more 🔦 at the next store.

How many total 🔦 did Izzy see?

_____

One shelf has 18 📖 .

Another shelf has 6 📖 .

How many total 📖 ?

_____

Help Izzy organize.

Cut out each object below.
Then, sort them into two categories. Glue or tape each group into a closet.
Then, label each closet with the name of the category.

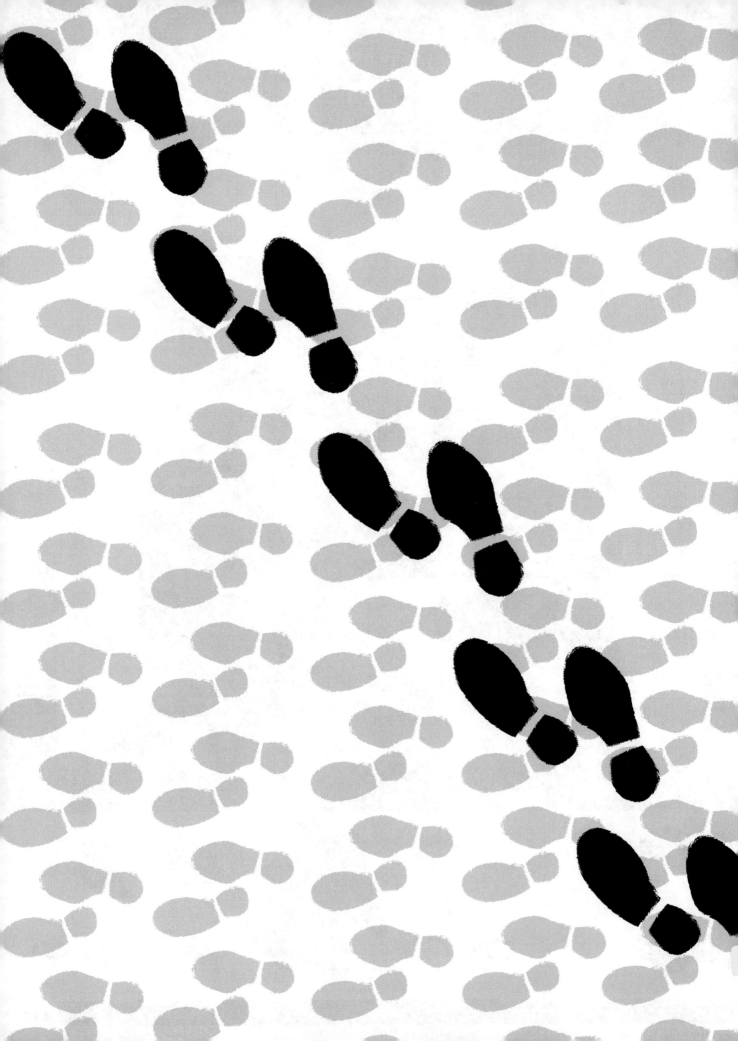

Subtract. Cross out tens blocks to help you.

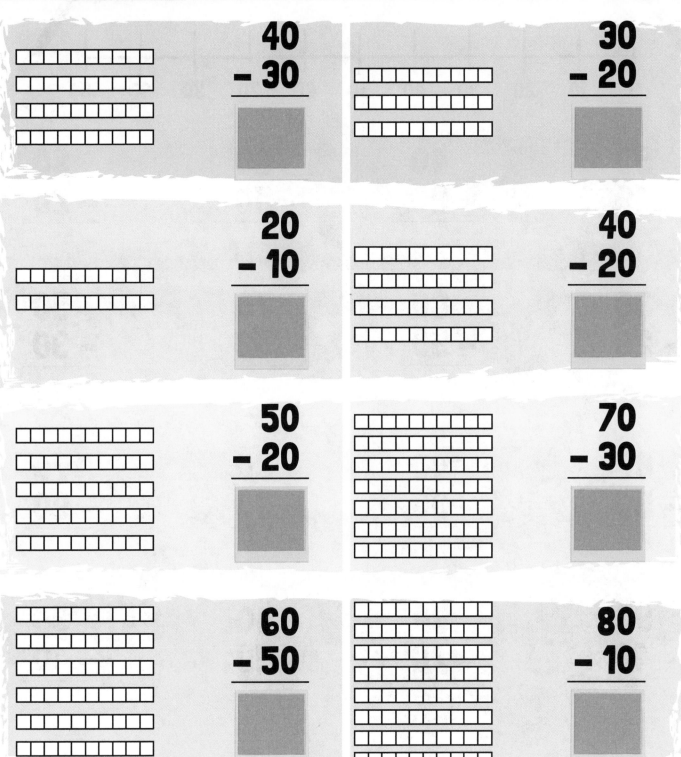

40
− 30
_____

30
− 20
_____

20
− 10
_____

40
− 20
_____

50
− 20
_____

70
− 30
_____

60
− 50
_____

80
− 10
_____

Subtract. Use the number line to help you.

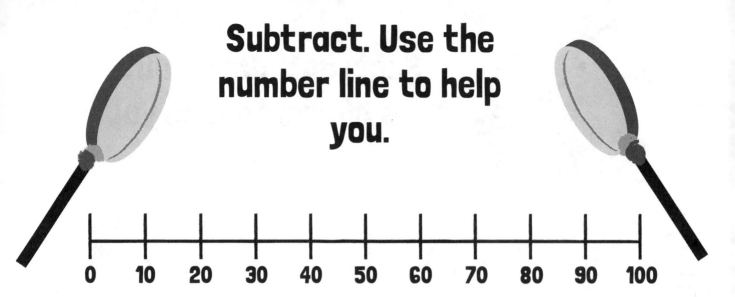

50 – 10	40 – 20	60 – 10	80 – 20
30 – 20	60 – 50	70 – 50	50 – 30
80 – 50	40 – 30	60 – 30	70 – 20
90 – 10	80 – 70	40 – 10	90 – 40

Help Izzy develop the pictures.
Circle the verb in each sentence.
Then, draw a picture that shows the action.

Izzy hops on one foot.

Charlie walks to the park.

Izzy rides her bike.

The cat sleeps on the chair.

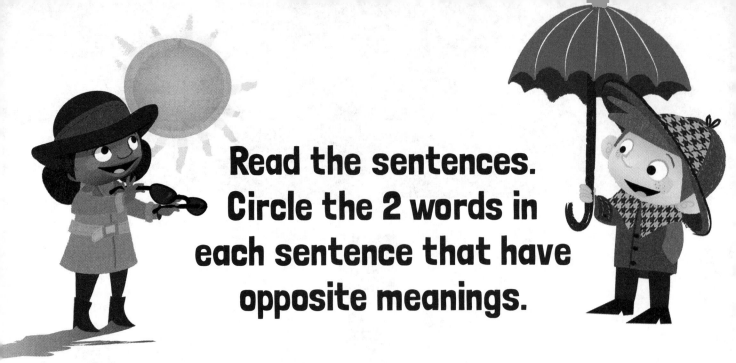

Read the sentences.
Circle the 2 words in
each sentence that have
opposite meanings.

A tiny dog found a huge bone.

My brother wiped his dirty hands on a clean towel.

The plane flew high in the sky and made a low sound.

Please close the window after you open the door.

I liked the first part of the book better than
the last part.

I would rather sit on a soft pillow than a hard chair.

Someone stole the hands from these clocks! Draw hands on each clock to show the time.

7:00

9:30

1:30

4:30

12:00

4:00

3:30

10:00

Help solve the case of the missing verbs! Write a verb to complete each sentence.

The frog _____ .

The pig _____ .

The fox _____ .

The fish _____ .

The duck _____ .

The dog _____ .

Match each shape to an object in the picture. Draw a line to connect them.

Read the sentences. Circle the nouns. Draw a line under the verbs.

The horse runs fast.

The car drives by my house.

Charlie plays with a yo-yo.

The squirrel eats a cookie.

Izzy looks for clues.

Help Izzy solve these problems.

There are 40 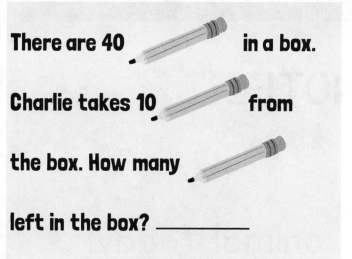 in a box. Charlie takes 10 from the box. How many left in the box? _____

The store has 70 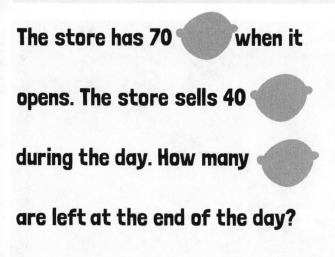 when it opens. The store sells 40 during the day. How many are left at the end of the day?

_____

Pond A has 50  .

Pond B has 20 .

How many more are in Pond A?

_____

There are 60 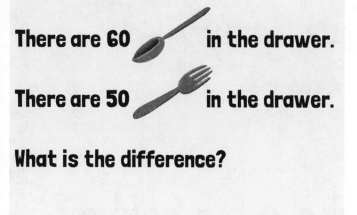 in the drawer.

There are 50 in the drawer.

What is the difference?

_____

Charlie has 80¢.

Izzy has 30¢.

What is the difference?

_____ ¢

Help Charlie edit his case notes.

One word in each sentence is misspelled.
Cross out the misspelled word. Write the correct spelling above it.

CASE NOTES

• •

I sau a strange animal today.

It had verry big ears.

Its skin wuz gray.

Its noes looked like a big snake.

CASE NOTES

Izzy sed it was not strange.

She told mee it was an elephant.

We were at the zew!

Draw a line from each shape to its name.

pyramid

sphere

cylinder

cone

cube

Adjectives are describing words. They tell what kind, how many, or what color. The adjectives in the sentences are in bold. Think of another adjective you might use. Write it on the line.

Izzy saw a **pretty** horse. _____

A **green** snake moved in the grass. _____

Charlie ate a **tasty** ice cream cone. _____

I picked a **plump** tomato from the garden. _____

There are **big** safes at the bank. _____

Earn your Spelling Detective badge! Circle the misspelled word in each sentence. Write the correct spelling on the line.

Izzy has too pairs of glasses.

_____

Charlie played checkers and one the game.

_____

A book was stolen frum the library.

_____

Izzy and Charlie our looking for clues.

_____

Wear did you put the flashlight?

_____

Sum people like to go fishing.

_____

The puppy is only for days old.

_____

Write the numbers to show the time on each watch.

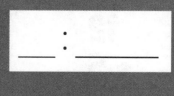

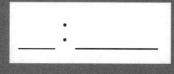

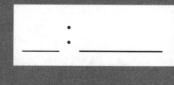

Add or subtract

12 + 5	21 + 7	30 − 10	42 + 7
80 − 20	45 + 9	22 + 8	18 − 9
80 + 9	45 + 6	70 − 30	90 − 40
20 − 8	39 + 4	25 + 8	57 + 6

Help Charlie and Izzy file their notes.

Cut out the words.
Then, put each word into
the correct file drawer.

noun   adjective   verb

table	cup	chase	clue	draw
tall	pig	round	jump	scary
green	eat	swim	wet	tub

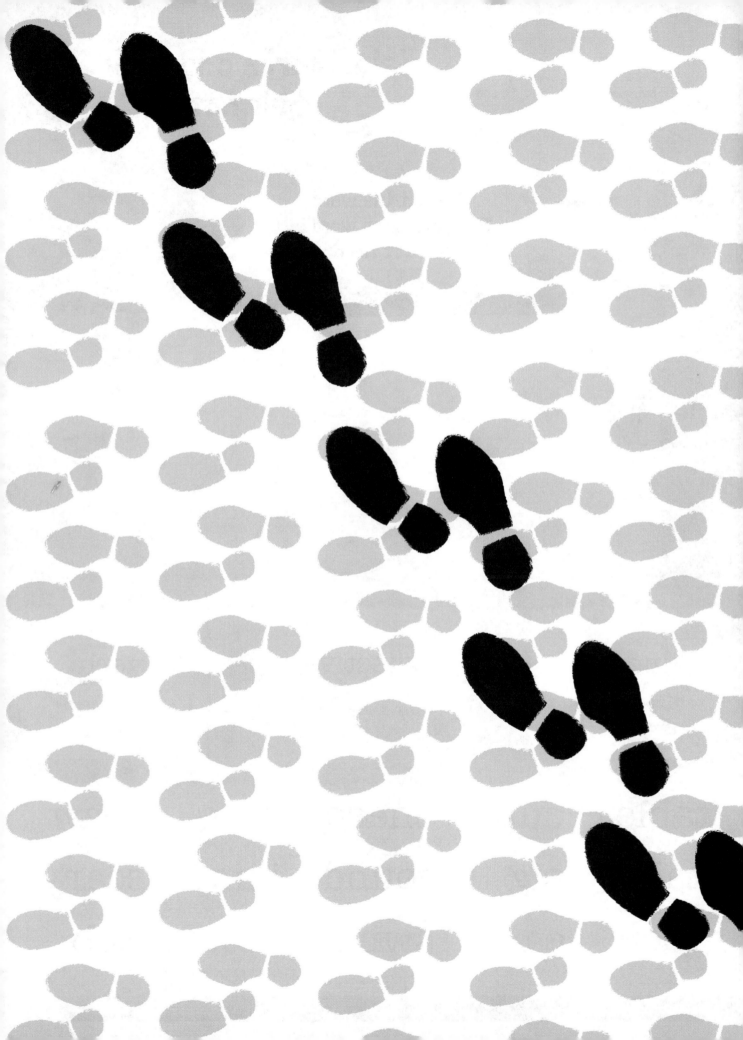

Label the shapes. Write **C** in all the circles. Write **R** in all the rectangles. Write **T** in all the triangles. Write **S** in all the squares.

Use the objects to help you test the equations. Circle the equations that are true.

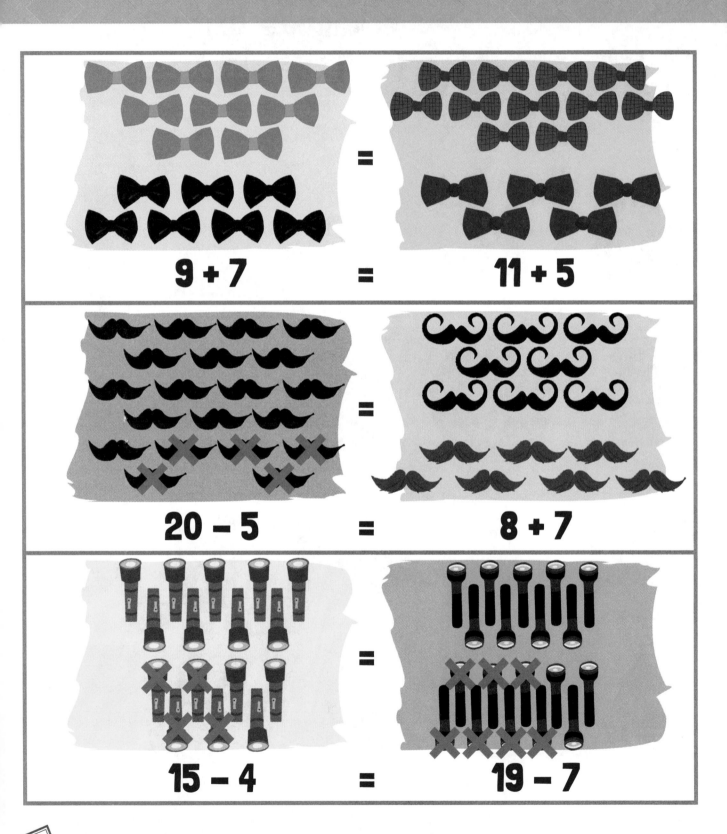

$9 + 7$ = $11 + 5$

$20 - 5$ = $8 + 7$

$15 - 4$ = $19 - 7$

Add an adjective to each sentence. Look at the pictures for ideas.

Izzy made a _____ snowman.

A _____ bus rumbled down the street.

I saw a _____ rainbow after the storm.

We ate _____ soup for lunch.

_____ turtles walked to the pond.

Help Charlie find the code to open the safe.

Circle the equations that are true. One equation is false. The 4 numbers of the false equation will open the safe.

$12 + 7 = 20 - 1$ $15 + 6 = 18 + 3$

$40 - 10 = 25 + 5$

$18 - 10 = 12 - 4$

$15 + 7 = 8 + 13$

$20 - 10 = 19 - 9$ $11 + 8 = 23 - 4$

$22 + 4 = 27 - 1$ $16 - 9 = 12 - 5$

five o'clock

12:00

four thirty

8:30

nine o'clock

1:30

eight thirty

Look at the picture.

Then, choose the preposition that correctly completes each sentence.

Charlie is _____ the lamppost.

behind   next to   from

Izzy is _____ the window.

above   on   in front of

The bird is _____ the building.

on top of   above   around

The robber is running _____ the door.

out   in   over

Please ____rite your name on the line.

Charlie gav____ his notes to Izzy.

She re____d the first page.

The frog sw____m across the pond.

Izzy got wet in the ra____n.

I put a vas____ of flowers on the table.

A w____rm dug into the dirt.

There are three fis____ in the tank.

Rewrite each addition problem as a subtraction problem. The first one has been done as an example.

12 + 9 = 21	21 − 9 = 12
24 + 5 = 29	29 − 5 = _____
15 + 7 = 22	22 − 7 = _____
33 + 4 = 37	37 − _____ = _____
27 + 6 = 33	33 − _____ = _____
40 + 8 = 48	48 − _____ = _____
35 + 7 = 42	42 − _____ = _____
23 + 9 = 32	32 − _____ = _____
37 + 4 = 41	41 − _____ = _____
42 + 9 = 51	51 − _____ = _____

Addition, Subtraction

Now, rewrite each subtraction problem as an addition problem. The first one has been done as an example.

22 − 8 = 14   14 + 8 = 22

27 − 5 = 22   22 + 5 = _____

21 − 7 = 14   14 + _____ = _____

30 − 6 = 24   24 + _____ = _____

33 − 4 = 29   29 + _____ = _____

41 − 5 = 36   36 + _____ = _____

35 − 9 = 26   26 + _____ = _____

19 − 9 = 10   10 + _____ = _____

27 − 8 = 19   19 + _____ = _____

32 − 5 = 27   27 + _____ = _____

The letters in each word are mixed up. Write each word correctly.

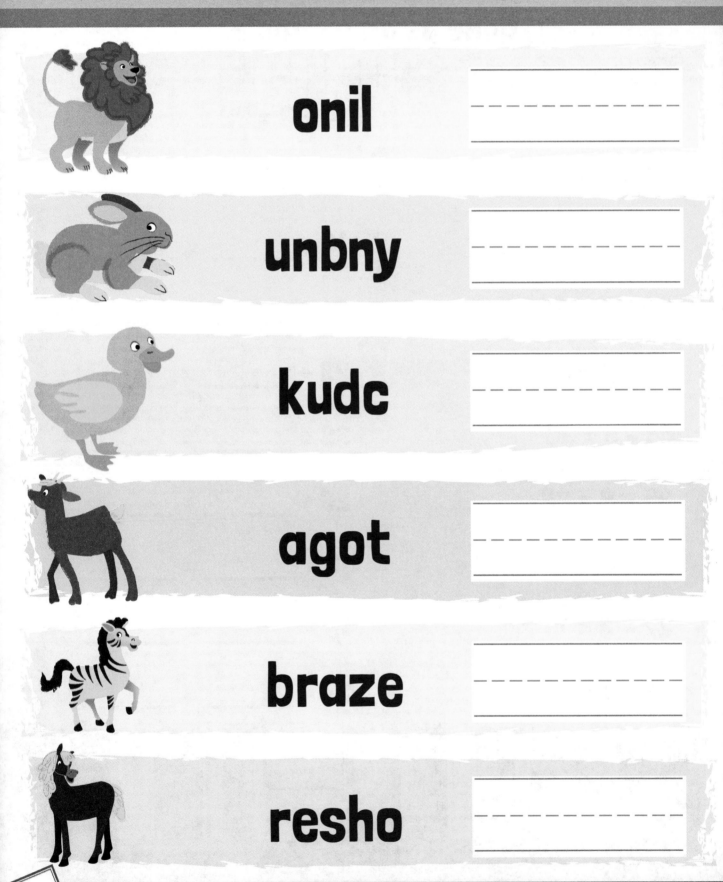

onil _____

unbny _____

kudc _____

agot _____

braze _____

resho _____

Help Charlie finish writing his case notes.

Add a prepositional phrase that answers the question Where?
The first one is done as an example.

CASE NOTES

I found a coin under the desk.

Izzy parked her bike

_____.

My coat is hanging

_____.

I hid the book

_____.

Izzy put her camera

_____.

Solve each equation.
Then, circle true or false.

9 + 3 = _____

8 + 4 = _____

9 + 3 = 8 + 4

true   false

---

10 + 3 = _____

9 + 5 = _____

10 + 3 = 9 + 5

true   false

---

20 – 7 = _____

19 – 16 = _____

20 – 7 = 19 – 16

true   false

---

14 – 4 = _____

16 – 6 = _____

14 – 4 = 16 – 6

true   false

---

9 + 8 = _____

18 – 2 = _____

9 + 8 = 18 – 2

true   false

---

19 – 5 = _____

11 + 3 = _____

19 – 5 = 11 + 3

true   false

Read each group of words. Place an X on the word that does not belong.

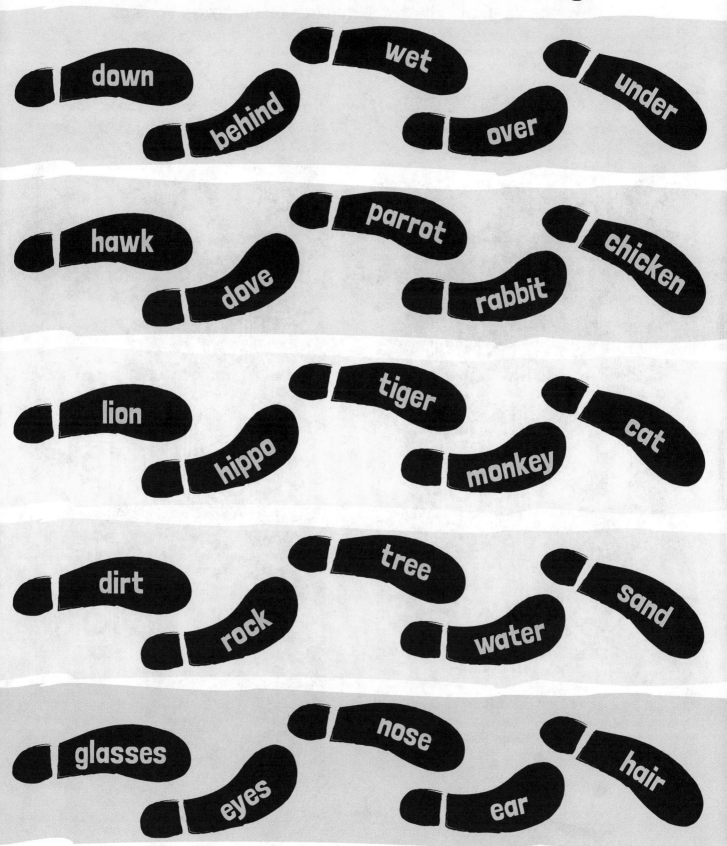

down
behind
wet
over
under

hawk
dove
parrot
rabbit
chicken

lion
hippo
tiger
monkey
cat

dirt
rock
tree
water
sand

glasses
eyes
nose
ear
hair

Charlie and Izzy are shopping for detective supplies.

Count the cameras in both cabinets. Then, write a number sentence to show the total number of cameras for sale.

_____ + _____ = _____

Count the magnifying glasses in both cabinets. Then, write a number sentence to show how many more are in the first cabinet.

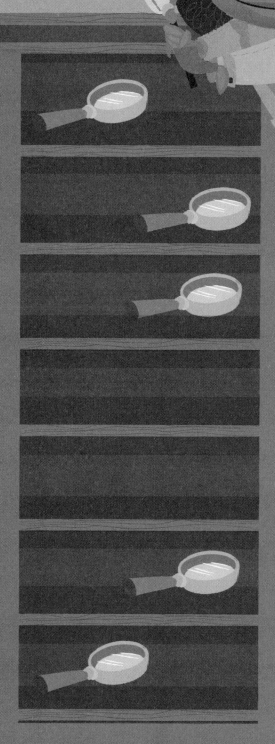

____ − ____ = ____

Read each sentence. Draw a picture to show how Izzy or Charlie feels.

Izzy enjoyed the cool breeze.

Izzy shivered in the icy breeze.

Charlie walked a small dog.

Charlie walked a tiny dog.

Charlie wore a _____ hat. (What kind?)

_____ dogs played at the park. (How many?)

Izzy's _____ coat is hanging in the closet. (Which one?)

The _____ fox hid behind the door. (Which one?)

I gave Izzy _____ keys that I found. (How many?)

A _____ car sped around the corner. (What kind?)

The _____ bird landed on top of a mailbox. (Which one?)

Charlie broke his _____ pair of sunglasses. (What kind?)

_____ children ran across the bridge. (How many?)

Some words sound the same, but they have different spellings and meanings.

Help Izzy choose the right word. Circle the word that correctly completes each sentence.

CASE NOTES

• •

_____ is Charlie going?

Wear   Where

I think he is walking _____ the store.

to   too

I wonder what he will _____ there?

by   buy

I hope it is a treat _____ me!

four   for

Cut out the shapes at the bottom of the page. Then, tape or glue each shape into the box that names it.

triangle	square
cube	cone
cylinder	rectangle
circle	pyramid
sphere	trapezoid

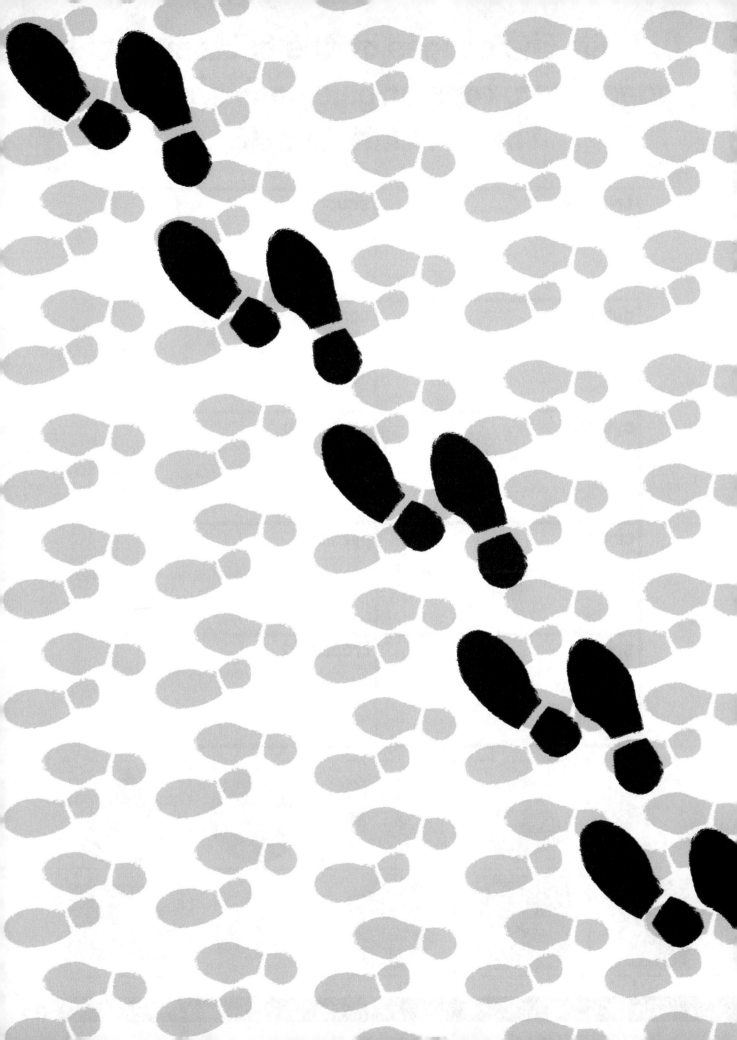

MONSTERS

Match the monsters.
Find 3 monsters that look alike.
Use the numbers on the 3 matching monsters to write a math problem.
You will need to write 2 addition problems and 2 subtractions problems.

___ + ___ = ___   ___ − ___ = ___

___ + ___ = ___   ___ − ___ = ___

Circle the sentences that tell about the past.

The monster cried.   The monster cries.

The monster waved.   The monster waves.

The monsters smile.   The monsters smiled.

The monster dances.   The monster danced.

The monster runs.   The monster ran.

Help the monsters move in.

Read each word.
Write the words in the rooms
where you think they go.

TV
couch
dresser
mirror

dishes
pans
books
computer

clothes
pillow
fruit
forks

The monster thinks all of his answers are correct.

Check his work to see. If an answer is wrong, cross it out. Then, write the correct answer.

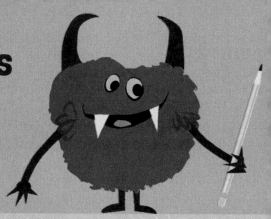

$$\begin{array}{r} 12 \\ + 8 \\ \hline 20 \end{array}$$

$$\begin{array}{r} 40 \\ - 20 \\ \hline 20 \end{array}$$

$$\begin{array}{r} 46 \\ + 5 \\ \hline 51 \end{array}$$

$$\begin{array}{r} 62 \\ + 7 \\ \hline 70 \end{array}$$

$$\begin{array}{r} 80 \\ - 20 \\ \hline 60 \end{array}$$

$$\begin{array}{r} 27 \\ + 4 \\ \hline 31 \end{array}$$

$$\begin{array}{r} 55 \\ + 2 \\ \hline 57 \end{array}$$

$$\begin{array}{r} 24 \\ + 8 \\ \hline 32 \end{array}$$

$$\begin{array}{r} 70 \\ - 40 \\ \hline 20 \end{array}$$

$$\begin{array}{r} 38 \\ + 5 \\ \hline 43 \end{array}$$

$$\begin{array}{r} 41 \\ + 9 \\ \hline 50 \end{array}$$

$$\begin{array}{r} 43 \\ + 6 \\ \hline 48 \end{array}$$

Many present-tense verbs are changed to past tense by adding -ed. Add -ed to the following verbs to make them past tense.

climb_____

wash_____

play_____

open_____   watch_____

help_____   clean_____

look_____   talk_____

If the present-tense verb already ends with -e, then just add -d. Add -d to the following verbs to make them past tense.

rake_____   close_____   hike_____

bake_____   chase_____   care_____

hope_____   save_____   share_____

Read the times. Draw the hands and write the numbers for each given time.

five thirty

three o'clock

nine thirty

The monsters are visiting the city.
They see lots of signs, but they see lots of mistakes, too.

Circle the misspelled words. Write the correct spellings on the lines below.

TOODAY'S SPECIAL:
Dog Food ½ price

BY SOME TODAY!

Save
BIG
at
BIG
Bob's!

Candee
Shop

Frank's Cheese Stoer

Toys Four Sale Inside!

HELP WONTED

Music Shop

_____

_____

_____

Look at each figure. Decide if the monster can roll it, stack it, or do both. Circle the answer(s).

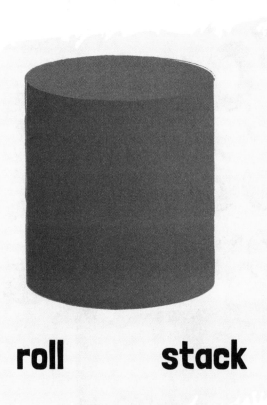

roll   stack

roll   stack

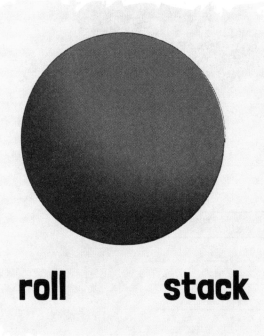

roll   stack

roll   **stack**

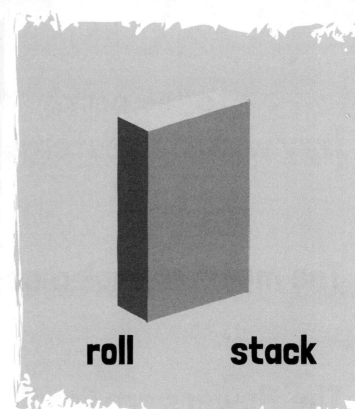

roll   **stack**

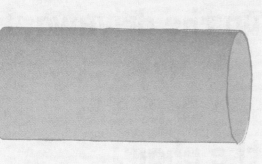

roll   **stack**

Use a ^ to add the phrase in parentheses to the sentence. The first one is done as an example.

to the park
Izzy walked ^ yesterday.   (to the park)

The monster took a cookie.   (from the jar)

The flowers are for Mom.   (in the vase)

Charlie rode his bike.   (up the driveway)

The cat is asleep.   (on the chair)

The monster is jumping.   (with three eyes)

Circle the past-tense verb on each kite.

see
saw

went
go

was
is

eat
ate

do
did

are
were

have
had

came
come

bit
bite

lost
lose

$$\begin{array}{r} 8 \\ + \;\square \\ \hline 15 \end{array}$$

$$\begin{array}{r} \square \\ + \;6 \\ \hline 15 \end{array}$$

$$\begin{array}{r} 12 \\ + \;\square \\ \hline 19 \end{array}$$

$$\begin{array}{r} \square \\ + \;5 \\ \hline 13 \end{array}$$

$$\begin{array}{r} 15 \\ + \;\square \\ \hline 20 \end{array}$$

$$\begin{array}{r} \square \\ + \;7 \\ \hline 18 \end{array}$$

$13 + \square = 20$

$\square + 10 = 20$

A strong breeze closed/slammed the door shut.

After the race, the runners quickly gulped/sipped cups of water.

Izzy felt great/okay about winning the writing contest.

The team scored, and the crowd screamed/said, "Hooray!"

My clothes were damp/soaked when I got caught in the heavy downpour.

Write the color name for each monster. Cross out letters in the box as you use them. The letters that are left will spell one more color. Write the color, and draw a monster to match it.

l r g r l u n d e w
l e e p e y p r o e

_____

_____

_____

_____

Welcome to the Monster Museum of Art.

Cut out the titles below.
Glue or tape each title next to the artwork it describes.

Two Faces

Six Sides

One Face

Three Angles

No Angles

Sometimes sentences have 2 verbs. Circle the verbs in each sentence.

The monster smiled and waved his arms.

The monster saw a bird and pointed at it.

The monster climbed into his bed and slept.

The monster made a sandwich and ate it.

Izzy ran and played at the park.

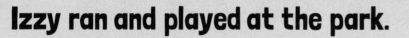

Use context clues to make the best choice for each red word's meaning.

Circle your choice.

The monsters were ecstatic about the new swimming pool. They smiled and roared, "New pool!" Then, they jumped in and played.

empty   happy   pretty

One monster fell down in the yard during lunch. She hurt her arm. The ache got worse when she tried to swim again.

dream   water   pain

Please listen now. I don't want to have to repeat this later.

say again   think about   leave

The monsters' clocks are all wrong. Each clock is a half hour slow. Draw hands on the blank clocks to show a half hour later. The first one has been done for you.

Write the correct present- or past-tense verb in the blank.

Last year, the monster_____when it was time to take a bath.

cries   cried

Now, the monster _____ taking baths.

loved   loves

He _____ clean and fresh whenever he takes a bath.

felt   feels

After his bath last night, the monster _____ great.

smells   smelled

The monster always _____ when he scrubs his toes.

giggles   giggled

Help the monster spot the mistakes. Circle the misspelled word in each set. Then, write the correct spelling.

man	boi	woman	- - - - - - - - -
doctor	chiled	teacher	- - - - - - - - -
fish	frog	gote	- - - - - - - - -
shurt	dress	shoes	- - - - - - - - -
threa	four	five	- - - - - - - - -
green	bloo	yellow	- - - - - - - - -
lion	hors	monkey	- - - - - - - - -
chiar	lamp	couch	- - - - - - - - -

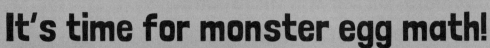

It's time for monster egg math!

Solve each problem. Then, help Charlie get to Izzy.
Starting at the egg with the arrow, draw a line
connecting the eggs with the same answers.

$$\begin{array}{r} 42 \\ +\ 8 \\ \hline \end{array}$$

$$\begin{array}{r} 33 \\ +\ 7 \\ \hline \end{array}$$

$$\begin{array}{r} 12 \\ +\ 9 \\ \hline \end{array}$$

$$\begin{array}{r} 50 \\ -10 \\ \hline \end{array}$$

$$\begin{array}{r} 70 \\ -20 \\ \hline \end{array}$$

$$\begin{array}{r} 46 \\ +\ 4 \\ \hline \end{array}$$

$$\begin{array}{r} 62 \\ +\ 3 \\ \hline \end{array}$$

$$\begin{array}{r} 44 \\ +\ 7 \\ \hline \end{array}$$

$$\begin{array}{r} 29 \\ +\ 8 \\ \hline \end{array}$$

Addition, Subtraction

$$\begin{array}{r} 14 \\ + 9 \\ \hline \end{array}$$

$$\begin{array}{r} 60 \\ -20 \\ \hline \end{array}$$

$$\begin{array}{r} 38 \\ - 2 \\ \hline \end{array}$$

$$\begin{array}{r} 55 \\ - 5 \\ \hline \end{array}$$

$$\begin{array}{r} 27 \\ + 5 \\ \hline \end{array}$$

$$\begin{array}{r} 36 \\ + 8 \\ \hline \end{array}$$

$$\begin{array}{r} 70 \\ -30 \\ \hline \end{array}$$

$$\begin{array}{r} 41 \\ + 9 \\ \hline \end{array}$$

$$\begin{array}{r} 90 \\ -40 \\ \hline \end{array}$$

Write each verb in the correct column.

slept   smiles   sang   take   found
hid   sees   plays   flew   carry

Yesterday	Today
_____	_____
_____	_____
_____	_____
_____	_____
_____	_____

Expand each sentence by writing a second verb on the line.

Izzy dances and _____ for her friends.

Please close the door and _____.

The ball bounces and _____.

The cup fell off the table and _____.

Charlie played and _____ at the park.

The ice cracks and _____ in spring.

I turn off the light and _____.

$$\begin{array}{r} 19 \\ -\ \boxed{} \\ \hline 12 \end{array} \qquad \begin{array}{r} \boxed{} \\ -\ 4 \\ \hline 13 \end{array} \qquad \begin{array}{r} 15 \\ -\ \boxed{} \\ \hline 7 \end{array}$$

$$\begin{array}{r} \boxed{} \\ -\ 9 \\ \hline 10 \end{array} \qquad \begin{array}{r} 13 \\ -\ \boxed{} \\ \hline 5 \end{array} \qquad \begin{array}{r} \boxed{} \\ -\ 18 \\ \hline 2 \end{array}$$

$$17 - \boxed{} = 7 \qquad \boxed{} - 8 = 11$$

Help the monsters add commas (,).

Commas separate the items in a list in a sentence.
Add a comma below each monster.
One has been done for you.

I like to have eggs, toast and juice

for breakfast.

Reading soccer and drawing are

my hobbies.

We went to the store the

library and the park today.

Solve each equation.
Use the tens blocks
for help. Then, circle
True or False.

40 + 40 = _____

80 – 30 = _____

20 + 50 = _____

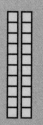 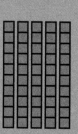

90 – 40 = _____

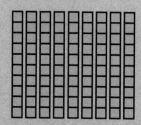

40 + 40 = 20 + 50

true   false

80 – 30 = 90 – 40

true   false

How many eyes in all? Write the equation shown by the 10-eyed monsters and the 1-eyed monsters.

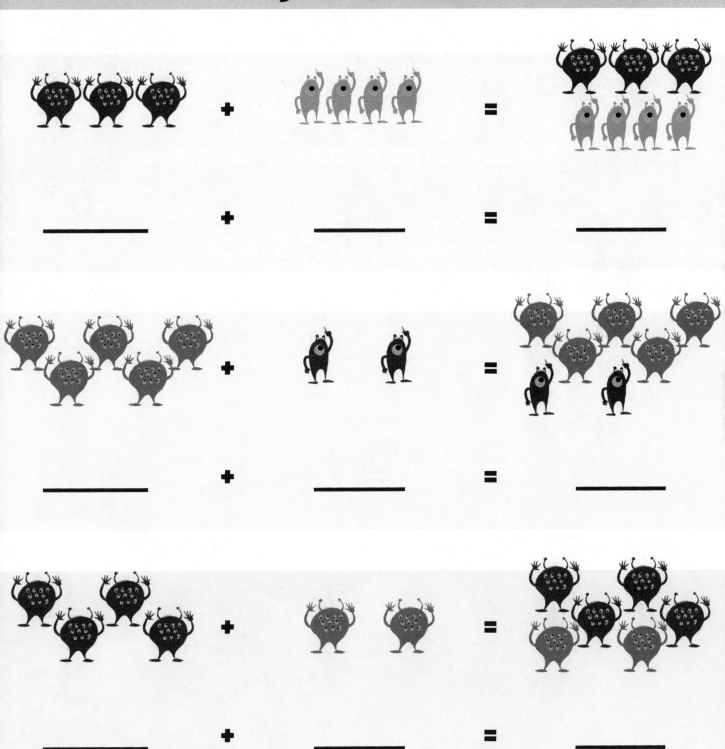

_____ + _____ = _____

_____ + _____ = _____

_____ + _____ = _____

Use context clues to make the best choice for each yellow word's meaning.

Circle your choice.

The monsters hoped there would be no precipitation today, but it stormed anyway, and they all got wet.

a bad day   rain or snow   umbrellas

Please speak up. I can't hear you when you mumble.

talk quietly   eat   walk away

Would you prefer to wear the pink shirt or the striped shirt?

clean   put away   like better

Help the monster find the right shapes. Color the shape that fits each description.

no faces

four equal sides

six equal faces

two faces are circles

no sides

When you add the helping verb will, you tell about what will happen later.

Add the helping verb will to complete each future tense verb.

Tomorrow, the monster _____ drive to the beach.

He _____ swim in the ocean.

He _____ play in the sand.

Write 2 sentences telling about something you will do in the future. Then, draw a picture of what you will do.

I will _____ .

I will _____ .

Solve.

There are 53 .

There are 7 .

How many 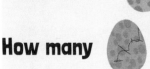 and total?

_____

There are 47 .

There are 8 .

How many and total?

_____

There were 70 .

The monsters ate 40 .

How many are left?

_____

60 came to a party.

30 more came to the party.

How many are at the party

now? _____

50 rode on a bus.

40 got off the bus.

how many are still on the

bus? _____

There were 80 at the park.

Then 60 left the park.

How many are at the park

now? _____

Cut out the sentence parts. Then, match a part from the left to a part from the right to make compound sentences.

and then he went to sleep.

The monster was hungry,

Charlie loves his new hat,

but it was not my birthday.

and he was very friendly.

I met a monster named Gordon,

I saw a gift with my name on it,

but Izzy thinks it looks silly.

so he ate a sandwich.

The monster read a book,

Fill in the missing number to complete each equation.

$$\begin{array}{r} 30 \\ + \boxed{} \\ \hline 38 \end{array} \qquad \begin{array}{r} \boxed{} \\ + 9 \\ \hline 29 \end{array} \qquad \begin{array}{r} 50 \\ + \boxed{} \\ \hline 55 \end{array}$$

$$\begin{array}{r} \boxed{} \\ + 60 \\ \hline 70 \end{array} \qquad \begin{array}{r} 50 \\ + \boxed{} \\ \hline 90 \end{array} \qquad \begin{array}{r} \boxed{} \\ + 40 \\ \hline 80 \end{array}$$

$$20 + \boxed{} = 90$$

$$\boxed{} + 8 = 78$$

The monster left his house at 1:00 to run errands.

home

bank

post office

grocery store

scream & shop grossery

park

a. monster
745 elm street
Boolane, IN 00000

Ms. Mary Very Scary
2016 AAAAGGHHH Drive
Underthebedopolis, MN, 00000

On the lines, write the times when he got to each place.

bank _____ : _____   grocery store _____ : _____

post office _____ : _____   park _____ : _____

How long did it take to go from home to the park? _____

Add a verb to tell about each picture. Use the tense shown in parentheses ( ).

Izzy _____ from Charlie.
(past)

Charlie _____ in a chair.
(present)

The monster _____ cake on his
birthday.
(future)

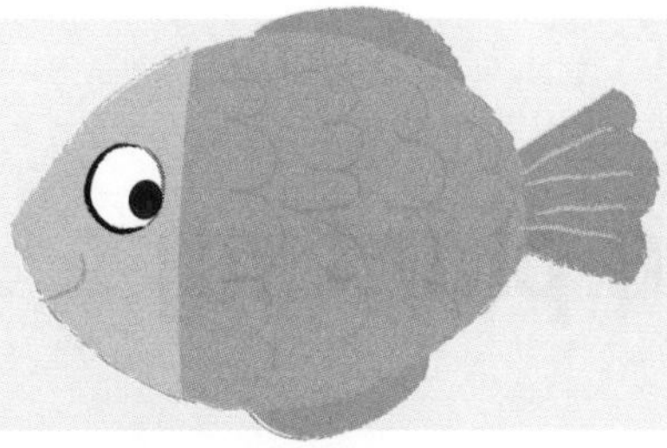

The fish _____ in the pond.
(present)

Charlie _____ to the store.
(past)

The monster _____ rope at
the park
(future)

The monster has a dog a cat and a bird as pets.

Lila Sam and Henry played a game.

I got a shirt a jacket and a pair of shoes at the store.

Mom Dad and Uncle Luis are planting flowers.

Maya put a cup bowl and spoon into the dishwasher.

The monster used paper scissors and paint to make a card.

Fill in the missing number to complete each equation.

$$90 - \boxed{} = 50$$

$$\boxed{} - 40 = 10$$

$$80 - \boxed{} = 55$$

$$\boxed{} - 30 = 20$$

$$90 - \boxed{} = 30$$

$$\boxed{} - 30 = 60$$

$$80 - \boxed{} = 60$$

$$\boxed{} - 0 = 50$$

Write 3 sentences to tell about the picture.

Help the monsters hunt for 3-D shapes. Find objects around you that match each shape. Draw a picture of what you find.

Commas are used in dates to separate the month and day from the year. Commas also separate the day of the week from the month and day. Add commas to the sentences below. The first 2 have been done as examples.

School starts on August 21 , 2017.

The play is on Friday , March 3.

My book is due Thursday   May 13.

The monster was born June 20   2012.

What holiday is on July 4   2018?

My party is planned for Tuesday   September 12.

Ruby missed school on February 15   2017.

We leave on Sunday   October 9.

Help Izzy solve these problems.

Write an equation for each problem. Then, solve.

You have 64 pennies.
You find 9 more.
How many pennies do you have total?

_____ + _____ = _____

A parking lot has 76 cars.
7 more cars park.
How many cars are in the lot now?

_____ + _____ = _____

A shop has 70 apples.
30 apples are sold.
How many apples are left?

_____ − _____ = _____

90 birds land in a tree.
Then 50 birds fly away.
How many birds are left?

_____ − _____ = _____

Tell the monster a bedtime math story! Think of a story problem for each equation. Draw a picture for the story. Then, fill in the missing number.

8
+ ☐
—
17

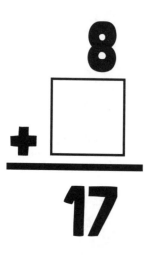

14
- ☐
—
9

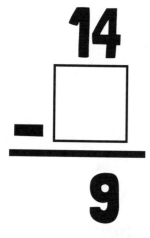

Circle the mistake in each sentence. Then, rewrite the sentence correctly.

There is a bike a scooter, and a ball in the shed.

_____

_____

_____

The monsters goes to the museum tomorrow.

_____

_____

_____

Izzy sau a bird in the tree.

_____

_____

_____

Write a word from the signs to answer each question. Use each word once.

sphere

cone

cube

pyramid

rectangular prism

cylinder

Which shape has four triangles for faces? _____

Which shape has a circle for its two faces? _____

Which shape has one circular face and one vertex (or "point")? _____

Which shape has six faces that are rectangles? _____

Which shape has six equal faces? _____

Which shape has no faces at all? _____

ANSWER KEY

Page 6

Write the vowel that completes each word.

a e i o u

ch **e** st   sh **i** p

h **a** t   b **u** g

cl **o** ck   fl **a** g

sh **e** ll   f **i** sh

Page 7

Say the name of each picture.

If it has a long a sound, color it green. If it has a short a sound, color it blue.

Page 8

Follow the directions.

1. Outline each circle.
2. Color each shape that has 4 sides.
3. Draw a dot in each square.
4. Draw an X on each shape with 3 sides.

Page 9

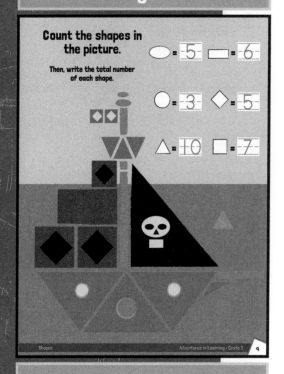

Count the shapes in the picture.

Then, write the total number of each shape.

⬭ = **5**   ▭ = **6**

◯ = **3**   ◇ = **5**

△ = **10**   □ = **7**

ANSWER KEY

Page 10

Say the name of each picture.

If it has a long e sound, circle it. If it has a short e sound, draw a square around it.

Page 11

Draw a line from the picture to the word that names it.

Draw a circle around the word if it has the long o sound.

pot

boat

dog

frog

goat

Page 12

Help Charlie solve each problem.

There are 3 .
Then, 4 more come.
Add to find the sum.

There are 6 .
two fly away.
How many are left?
4

Charlie has 7 .
Izzy has 4 .
What is the difference?
3

I have 8 .
I get 2 more .
What is 8 plus 2?
10

There are 5 .
Four swim away.
What is 5 minus 4?

There are 4 .
Then 4 more come.
How many in all?
8

Page 13

Help Izzy find the jewels.

Say the name of the picture on each chest. If it has the long i sound, the chest holds jewels. If it has the short i sound, the chest holds shells. Circle the chests with jewels.

ANSWER KEY

Page 14

Help Charlie add.

$4 + 6 = 10$ $5 + 2 = 7$

$6 + 4 = 10$ $2 + 5 = 7$

$3 + 4 = 7$ $3 + 6 = 9$

$4 + 3 = 7$ $6 + 3 = 9$

$\begin{array}{c} 2 \\ +6 \\ \hline 8 \end{array}$ $\begin{array}{c} 5 \\ +4 \\ \hline 9 \end{array}$ $\begin{array}{c} 10 \\ +0 \\ \hline 10 \end{array}$ $\begin{array}{c} 3 \\ +4 \\ \hline 7 \end{array}$ $\begin{array}{c} 7 \\ +2 \\ \hline 9 \end{array}$ $\begin{array}{c} 9 \\ +1 \\ \hline 10 \end{array}$

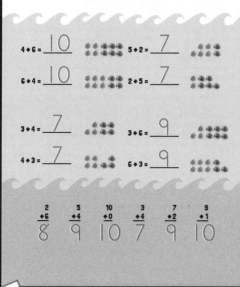

Page 15

Say the name of each picture.
If it has a long u sound, color it red. If it has a sound, color it yellow.

Page 16

Charlie and Izzy need supplies.
The list shows how many of each item they will take. Write the number next to the barrel, and cross out the same number of items. Then subtract to see how many are left. One has been done as an example.

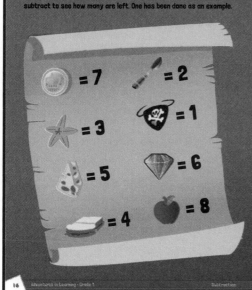

= 7   = 2

= 3   = 1

= 5   = 6

= 4   = 8

Page 17

$\begin{array}{c} 10 \\ -7 \\ \hline 3 \end{array}$ $\begin{array}{c} 10 \\ -2 \\ \hline 8 \end{array}$

$\begin{array}{c} 10 \\ -3 \\ \hline 7 \end{array}$ $\begin{array}{c} 10 \\ -1 \\ \hline 9 \end{array}$

$\begin{array}{c} 10 \\ -5 \\ \hline 5 \end{array}$ $\begin{array}{c} 10 \\ -6 \\ \hline 4 \end{array}$

$\begin{array}{c} 10 \\ -4 \\ \hline 6 \end{array}$ $\begin{array}{c} 10 \\ -8 \\ \hline 2 \end{array}$

ANSWER KEY

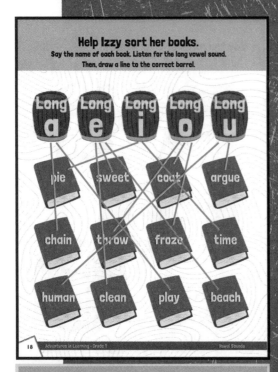

Help Izzy sort her books.
Say the name of each book. Listen for the long vowel sound.
Then, draw a line to the correct barrel.

Long a, Long e, Long i, Long o, Long u

pie, sweet, coat, argue
chain, throw, froze, time
human, clean, play, beach

Page 18

Subtract to find out how many ships are left.

8 − 2 = 6   7 − 3 = 4

9 − 6 = 3   10 − 7 = 3

6 − 1 = 5   6 − 6 = 0

8 − 3 = 5   8 − 5 = 3

Page 19

Help Izzy solve each problem.

There are 8 .
There are 2 .
How many more ___ than ___ are there? 6

Charlie buys ___ for 7¢.
He buys ___ for 3¢.
How much money did he spend? 10¢

There are 9 .
One ___ walks away.
How many are left? 8

An island has 4 .
Another island has 3 .
What is the sum? 7

Charlie has 10¢.
He buys ___ for 8¢.
How much money does he have left? 2¢

Izzy has 5¢.
She finds 3¢ more.
How much money does she have? 8¢

Page 20

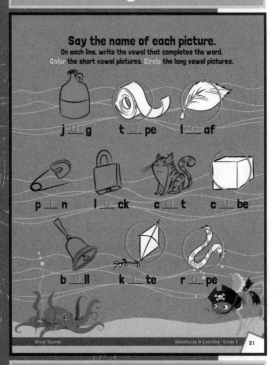

Say the name of each picture.
On each line, write the vowel that completes the word.
Color the short vowel pictures. Circle the long vowel pictures.

j u g   t a pe   l e af

p i n   l o ck   c a t   c u be

b e ll   k i te   r o pe

Page 21

ANSWER KEY

Page 22

Choose the vowel team to complete each word. Fill in the blanks.

s a i l
ai ee ay

b oa t
oo ow oa

b oo ts
oo ow oa

p ea s
ay ea ee

f ee t
ea ee ai

h ay
ai ay oa

sp oo n
ea oa oo

sn ow
ow oa

Page 23

A noun is a word that names a person, place, or thing.

Cut out the nouns below. Then, sort them into the correct boxes.

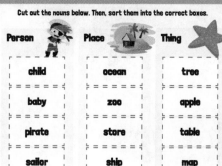

Person	Place	Thing
child	ocean	tree
baby	zoo	apple
pirate	store	table
sailor	ship	map

Page 25

Add or subtract.

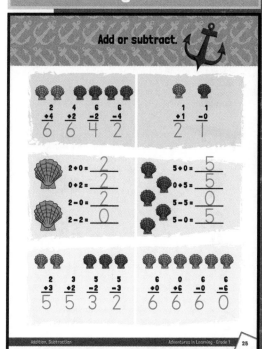

2 +4 = 6
4 +2 = 6
6 -2 = 4
6 -4 = 2

1 +1 = 2
1 -0 = 1

2+0 = 2
0+2 = 2
2-0 = 2
2-2 = 0

5+0 = 5
0+5 = 5
5-5 = 0
5-0 = 5

2 +3 = 5
3 +2 = 5
5 -2 = 3
5 -3 = 2

6 +0 = 6
0 +6 = 6
6 -0 = 6
6 -6 = 0

Page 26

A blend is made by combining two consonant sounds (Example: floor).

The name of each picture below begins with a blend. Circle the beginning blend for each picture.

bl
fl
(cl)

cl
(fl)
gl

fl
cl
(gl)

(dr)
br
tr

dr
(tr)
br

tr
dr
(br)

ANSWER KEY

Page 27

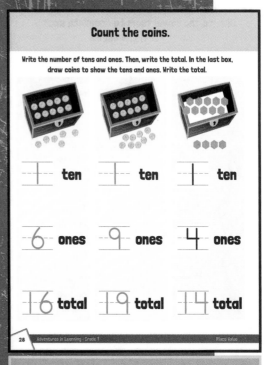

Page 28

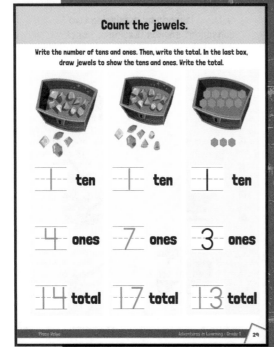

Page 29

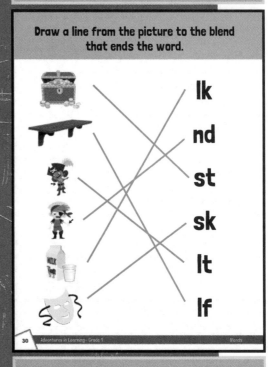

Page 30

ANSWER KEY

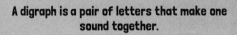

Page 31

A digraph is a pair of letters that make one sound together.

Name each picture. Listen for the digraphs ch, sh, and th. If the name begins with a diagraph, circle the picture. If the name ends with a diagraph, underline the picture.

Page 32

Help Charlie catch the stowaways!
Cross out the word on each ship that does not belong.

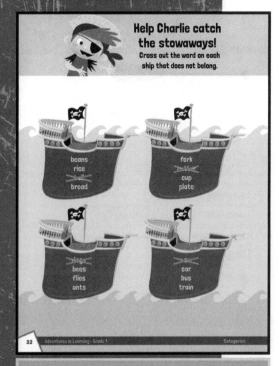

Page 33

Count the tens and ones.
Then, write the number. The first one is done for you.

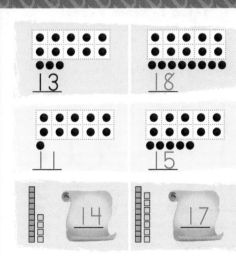

Page 34

Number the boats as follows:
1 - long, 2 - medium, 3 - short.

ANSWER KEY

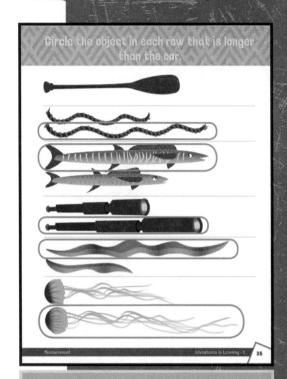

Page 35

Page 36

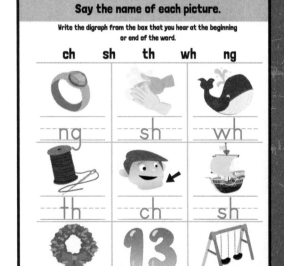

Page 37

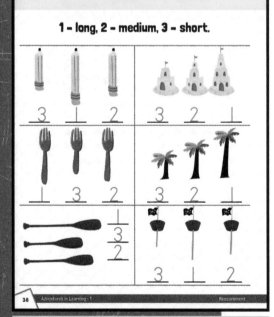

Page 38

ANSWER KEY

Add or subtract.

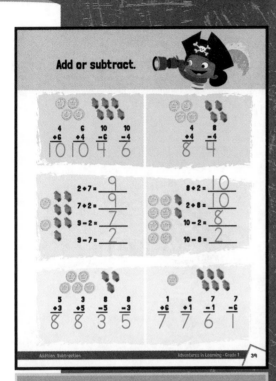

Page 39

$1+3 = 4$ $4-3 = 1$ $4+5 = 9$

$6+2 = 8$ $7-2 = 5$ $8-5 = 3$

$9-4 = 5$ $10-5 = 5$

$4+3 = 7$

$6+3 = 9$

$8+2 = 10$ $10-3 = 7$

Page 40

Help Charlie organize the hold.
Circle the object on each shelf that does not belong.

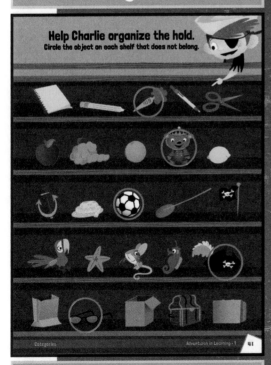

Page 41

Write words from the box on the flags that describe them.

| Izzy | four | Max | cat | dog | yellow |
| blue | red | pig | Charlie | two | one |

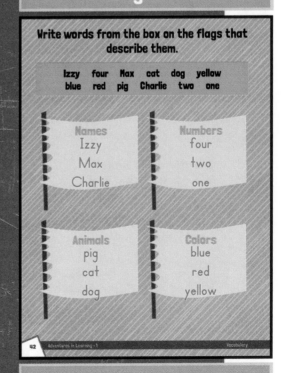

Names
Izzy
Max
Charlie

Numbers
four
two
one

Animals
pig
cat
dog

Colors
blue
red
yellow

Page 42

ANSWER KEY

Page 43

Draw shapes to fit each rule.

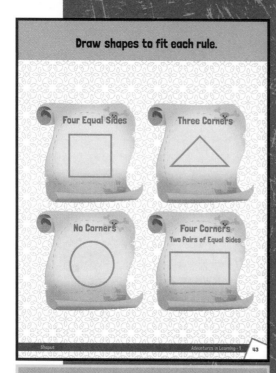

Four Equal Sides

Three Corners

No Corners

Four Corners
Two Pairs of Equal Sides

Page 44

Help Izzy find the answers to these problems.

7 + 3 = 10   5 − 2 = 3   3 + 6 = 9

2 + 7 = 9   6 − 3 = 3   9 − 5 = 4

4 − 4 = _____   10 − 7 = 3   3 + 2 = 5

4 + 2 = _____

10 − 4 = _____

8 − 7 = _____

Page 45

Circle the word in each row that is most like the first word in the row.

bee   fish   (ant)   snake
grin   (smile) frown mad
bag   jar   (sack) box
bird   dog   cat   (duck)
ship   (boat) bike   car
round square (ball) star

Page 46

Help Izzy build a castle!
First, circle the correct name of each shape below.
Then, use the shapes to make a castle on the next page.
Use each shape as often as you need.

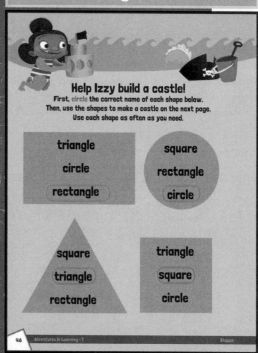

triangle
circle
(rectangle)

square
(rectangle)
circle

square
(triangle)
rectangle

triangle
(square)
circle

ANSWER KEY

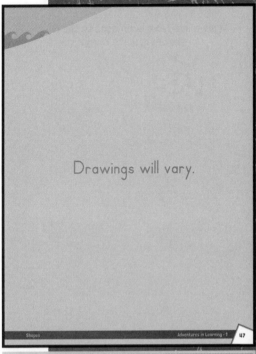

Drawings will vary.

Page 47

Read each sentence and look at the underlined word.

Circle the word that means almost the same thing.

Charlie is a <u>nice</u> pirate.   mad **(kind)** bad

The bird is in the <u>tall</u> tree.   green   pretty **(big)**

Izzy is <u>tired</u>.   **(sleepy)** sad   little

The <u>little</u> fish swam.   tall   funny **(small)**

The <u>quick</u> crab ran.   slow   mean **(fast)**

The <u>happy</u> girl smiled.   **(glad)** sad   good

Page 48

When you read a sentence, a noun is what the sentence is about.

Complete each sentence below with a noun.

The **fish** is tiny.
small   fish   swim

The **bird** is green.
funny   stop   bird

The **ship** is sailing.
float   ship   big

The **sun** is hot.
sun   shine   yellow

Page 49

An s at the end of a noun usually means it is plural, or shows more than one.

Look at each group. Circle the correct word.

dolphin **(dolphins)**

pail **(pails)**

shell **(shells)**

chest **(chests)**

(tree) trees

Page 50

ANSWER KEY

Page 51

Help Izzy count to 20.
Write the number that is hidden under each object.

1	2	3	4	5
6	7	🦞	9	10
🧭	12	13	👑	15
16	🎩	18	⚓	20

🦞 = 8

🧭 = 11

👑 = 14

🎩 = 17

⚓ = 19

Page 52

Draw a line from each boat to the noun that names its cargo.

balls   flags   cat   stars

Page 53

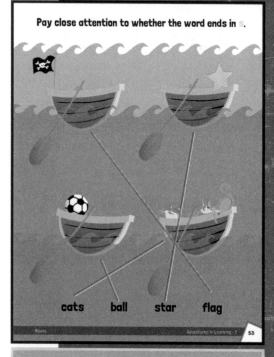

Pay close attention to whether the word ends in s.

cats   ball   star   flag

Page 54

Color the 6 fish. From smallest to biggest, use these colors: green, red, blue, orange, yellow, purple.

ANSWER KEY

Charlie and Izzy are counting their jewels, but they missed 6 numbers.

Write the missing numbers.

1	2	3	4	5	6	7	8	9	10
27 11	12	13	14	15	16	17	18	19	20
35 21	22	23	24	25	26	27	28	29	30
44 31	32	33	34	35	36	37	38	39	40
59 41	42	43	44	45	46	47	48	49	50
63 51	52	53	54	55	56	57	58	59	60
61	62	63	64	65	66	67	68	69	70
92 71	72	73	74	75	76	77	78	79	80
81	82	83	84	85	86	87	88	89	90
91	92	93	94	95	96	97	98	99	100

Page 56

Proper nouns are names of particular people, places, things, or events. Proper nouns always begin with a capital letter.

Underline the proper noun in each sentence.

Please tell <u>Izzy</u> to walk the dog.

Let's bake a cake for <u>Charlie</u>.

His birthday is in <u>May</u>.

The dragon's name is <u>Daisy</u>.

The castle is near the town of <u>Royalton</u>.

What will you wear for <u>Halloween</u>?

Page 57

Write Charlie's name and Izzy's name. Then write your first and last name. Remember: names are proper nouns. Draw a picture of yourself in the box.

Izzy

Charlie

<u>Answers and</u>

<u>drawings will vary</u>.

Page 58

Help Izzy sort the animals into categories.

Cut out each animal name. Glue or tape it into the correct box.

Pet	Zoo	Pretend
beagle	hippo	unicorn
hamster	otter	troll
rabbit	elephant	dragon
canary	tiger	Bigfoot

Page 59

ANSWER KEY

Help Izzy use the number line to add!
Count on to solve each problem.

0 1 2 3 4 5 6 7 8 9 10 11 12 13 14 15 16 17 18 19 20

10	12	11	11	14	15
+ 8	+ 5	+ 7	+ 3	+ 2	+ 4
18	17	18	14	16	19

Addition   Adventures in Learning · 1   61

Page 61

Write a noun from the box to tell who is doing something in each sentence.

The __boy__ rode a horse.
boy   man   woman

The __children__ drank tea.
girls   children   men

The __girl__ smiled.
mother   girl   women

The __woman__ washed the happy dog.
woman   children   man

Some __people__ like to bake.
fathers   person   people

62   Adventures in Learning · 1   Nouns

Page 62

Help Charlie use the number line to subtract!
Count back to solve each problem.

0 1 2 3 4 5 6 7 8 9 10 11 12 13 14 15 16 17 18 19 20

20	19	16	13	16	14
− 8	− 5	− 3	− 7	− 8	− 12
12	14	13	6	8	2

Subtraction   Adventures in Learning · 1   63

Page 63

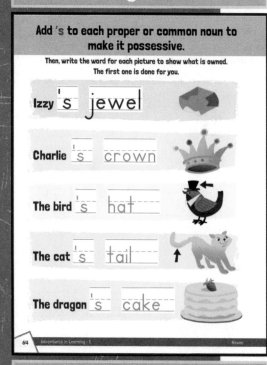

Add 's to each proper or common noun to make it possessive.

Then, write the word for each picture to show what is owned.
The first one is done for you.

Izzy __'s__ __jewel__

Charlie __'s__ __crown__

The bird __'s__ __hat__

The cat __'s__ __tail__

The dragon __'s__ __cake__

64   Adventures in Learning · 1   Nouns

Page 64

ANSWER KEY

Page 65

Help Charlie and Izzy count forward and backward. Write the missing numbers.

25, 26, **27**, 28, 29, **30**, 31, **32**, 33, **34**

48, **49**, 50, 51, 52, **53**, 54, **55**, **56**, 57

70, 71, 72, 73, **74**, **75**, 76, **77**, 78, 79

84, 85, 86, **87**, 88, **89**, 90, **91**, 92, **93**

32, 31, 30, **29**, 28, 27, **26**, **25**, 24, **23**

50, 49, 48, 47, **46**, 45, **44**, 43, **42**, 41

65, **64**, 63, 62, **61**, 60, **59**, 58, 57, **56**

81, **80**, 79, **78**, 77, 76, 75, **74**, **73**, 72

Place Value · Adventures in Learning · 1 · 65

Page 66

Charlie and Izzy are in the royal library. Some of the books are on the wrong shelves. Read the titles on each shelf. Circle the book with the word that does not belong.

Trains | Jets | Planes | Hands | Cars

Rose | Tulip | Trees | Daisy | Sunflower

Lake | Ocean | Chair | Pond | River

66 · Adventures in Learning · 1 · Vocabulary

Page 67

Blue | Red | Green | Square | Yellow

Park | Home | School | Happy | Castle

Horse | Dolphin | Shark | Whale | Seal

Small | Cold | Heavy | Tall | Short

Play | Run | Grass | Roll | Climb

Vocabulary · Adventures in Learning · Grade 1 · 67

Page 68

Help Charlie solve the problems.

There are 10 ☕.
There are 2 🫖.
How many ☕ and 🫖 total? **12**

There are 8 👑.
There are 6 👑.
How many crowns in all? **14**

There are 5 👗.
There are 7 👗.
How many dresses in all? **12**

Izzy puts 11 🍷 on the table.
Then she adds 3 more 🍷.
How many 🍷 in all? **14**

There are 9 🐦.
There are 4 🐦.
Find the total number of birds. **13**

There are 9 ⬤.
There are 4 🪶.
Find the total. **13**

68 · Adventures in Learning · 1 · Addition

ANSWER KEY

Page 69

Pronouns can be used in place of some nouns.

Write the pronoun He, She, or They in each sentence below.

Charlie likes cookies.

__He__ likes cookies.

Izzy drinks tea.

__She__ drinks tea.

Charlie and Izzy have good manners.

__They__ have good manners.

Page 70

Help Izzy find the secret path across the moat.

Look at each subtraction problem. The stones with wrong answers will sink! Find the path with correct answers.

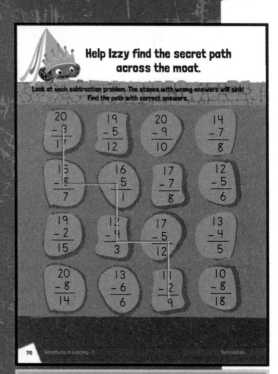

20 − 3 = 17	19 − 5 = 12	20 − 9 = 10	14 − 7 = 8
15 − 8 = 7	16 − 5 = 1	17 − 7 = 8	12 − 5 = 6
19 − 2 = 15	12 − 9 = 3	17 − 5 = 12	13 − 4 = 5
20 − 8 = 14	13 − 6 = 6	11 − 2 = 9	10 − 8 = 18

Page 71

Help Charlie find the answers to these problems.

9 + 5 = 14	11 − 6 = 5	12 + 7 = 19
12 + 3 = 15	16 − 6 = 10	9 + 7 = 16
15 − 4 = 11	18 − 7 = 11	
13 + 3 = 16	14 + 2 = 16	
10 − 9 = 1	11 + 4 = 15	

Page 72

Possessive pronouns tell who owns something.

Write a possessive pronoun from the box to replace each word in bold type.

her   my   his   their   its

Charlie's birthday = __his__ birthday

Charlie's and Izzy's jewels = __their__ jewels

the horse's tail = __its__ tail

the book belonging to me = __my__ book

Izzy's throne = __her__ throne

ANSWER KEY

Each goblet has 10 jewels. Count the tens.

Then, write the total number of jewels.

30   40

60

80

Page 73

Help Charlie choose the right pronouns.

Circle the pronoun that correctly completes each sentence.

Daisy the dragon is (our)/ours friend.

Her /(She) lives in a cave.

Sometimes I visit she's /(her) cave.

Izzy fed the horses (their)/theirs food.

Now (we)/us can ride to see Daisy!

Page 74

Each goblet has 10 jewels. Draw goblets to show each number.

The first one has been done for you.

50   20

10   30

Page 75

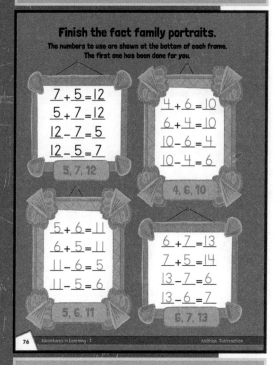

Finish the fact family portraits.

The numbers to use are shown at the bottom of each frame.
The first one has been done for you.

$7 + 5 = 12$
$5 + 7 = 12$
$12 - 7 = 5$
$12 - 5 = 7$

5, 7, 12

$4 + 6 = 10$
$6 + 4 = 10$
$10 - 6 = 4$
$10 - 4 = 6$

4, 6, 10

$5 + 6 = 11$
$6 + 5 = 11$
$11 - 6 = 5$
$11 - 5 = 6$

5, 6, 11

$6 + 7 = 13$
$7 + 5 = 14$
$13 - 7 = 6$
$13 - 6 = 7$

6, 7, 13

Page 76

ANSWER KEY

Page 77

Circle the correct noun, pronoun, or possessive to complete each sentence.

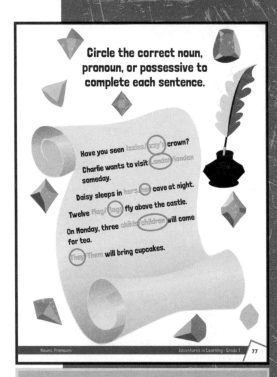

Have you seen Izzies/**Izzy's** crown?

Charlie wants to visit **London**/Londen someday.

Daisy sleeps in hers/**her** cave at night.

Twelve flag/**flags** fly above the castle.

On Monday, three childs/**children** will come for tea.

They/Them will bring cupcakes.

Page 78

Finish the fact family portraits.
The numbers to use are shown at the bottom of each frame.

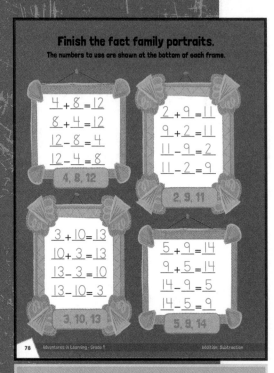

$4 + 8 = 12$
$8 + 4 = 12$
$12 - 8 = 4$
$12 - 4 = 8$

4, 8, 12

$2 + 9 = 11$
$9 + 2 = 11$
$11 - 9 = 2$
$11 - 2 = 9$

2, 9, 11

$3 + 10 = 13$
$10 + 3 = 13$
$13 - 3 = 10$
$13 - 10 = 3$

3, 10, 13

$5 + 9 = 14$
$9 + 5 = 14$
$14 - 9 = 5$
$14 - 5 = 9$

5, 9, 14

Page 79

Circle the correctly spelled word in each set. Then, write it on the lines.

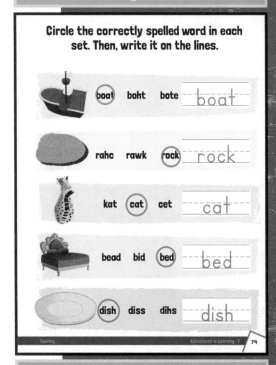

boat boht bote — boat

rahc rawk **rock** — rock

kat **cat** cet — cat

bead bid **bed** — bed

dish diss dihs — dish

Page 80

Circle the misspelled word in each set. Then, write the correct spelling on the line.

pet **dogg** brown — dog

yellow **berd** wing — bird

fork dish **spon** — spoon

cake **swete** pink — sweet

ball game **bloo** — blue

trea plant leaf — tree

ANSWER KEY

Read each sentence. Draw a picture to show how Izzy or Charlie feels.

Izzy was happy when the rain stopped.

Drawings will vary.

Izzy was thrilled when the sun came out.

Charlie saw a big spider.

Charlie saw a gigantic spider.

Page 81

Help Izzy measure. She is using spoons to measure the lengths. Write the measurement on each line.

The dog is about ___4___ spoons long.

The bird is about ___1___ spoon long.

Page 82

Each crown has 10 jewels. Count the groups of crowns, and write the number by the word tens. Count the other jewels, and write the number by the word ones. Then, write the total.

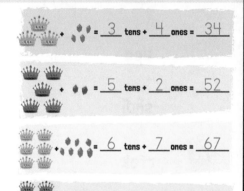

= ___3___ tens + ___4___ ones = ___34___

= ___5___ tens + ___2___ ones = ___52___

= ___6___ tens + ___7___ ones = ___67___

= ___8___ tens + ___5___ ones = ___85___

Page 83

Charlie is unsure what some of these words mean.

Draw a line from each red word to a word on the next page that has a more familiar meaning.

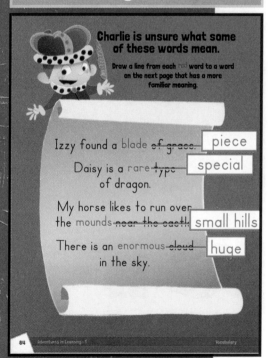

Izzy found a blade of grass. — piece

Daisy is a rare type of dragon. — special

My horse likes to run over the mounds near the castle. — small hills

There is an enormous cloud in the sky. — huge

Page 84

ANSWER KEY

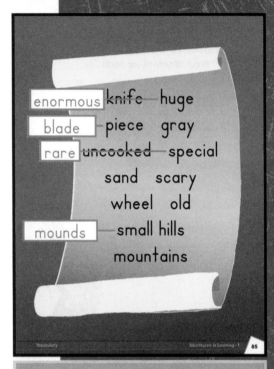

Page 85

enormous — knife   huge
blade — piece   gray
rare — uncooked — special
sand   scary
wheel   old
mounds — small hills
mountains

Page 86

Circle the shape of the bottom face of each figure.

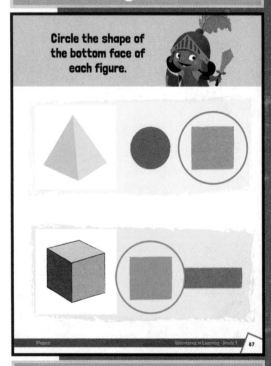

Page 87

Circle the shape of the bottom face of each figure.

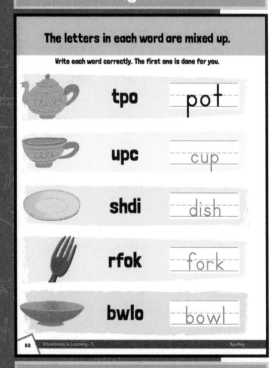

Page 88

The letters in each word are mixed up.

Write each word correctly. The first one is done for you.

	tpo	pot
	upc	cup
	shdi	dish
	rfok	fork
	bwlo	bowl

ANSWER KEY

Page 89

Cut out the line of coins.
Use the coins to measure each object.

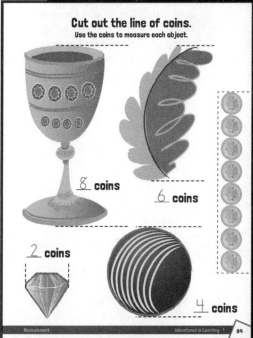

_8_ coins

_6_ coins

_2_ coins

_4_ coins

Page 91

Each sentence has one incorrect noun or pronoun. Circle the mistake. Write the correct noun or pronoun on the line.

Charlie ate (he's) lunch.	his
Please tell (izzy) to bring me my crown.	Izzy
Where is (yours) goblet?	your
Ten (flag) fly above the castle.	flags
The (horses) mane is very pretty.	horse's
(Mine) jewels are in the safe.	My
The baker made seven fancy (cake).	cakes

Page 92

Help Izzy and Charlie defend the kingdom.
Circle the shield with the number that matches each description.
Then, write the circled numbers from least to greatest.

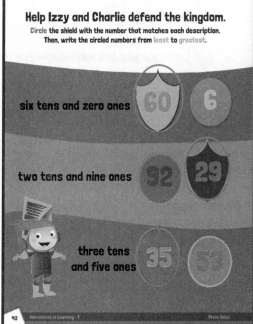

six tens and zero ones — 60 6

two tens and nine ones — 92 29

three tens and five ones — 35 53

Page 93

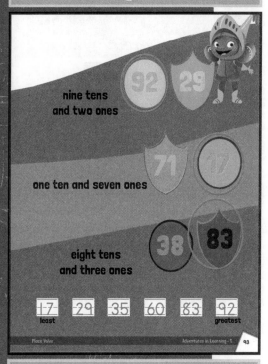

nine tens and two ones — 92 29

one ten and seven ones — 71 17

eight tens and three ones — 38 83

17	29	35	60	83	92
least					greatest

ANSWER KEY

Daisy is a strong dragon. Circle the word in each pair that has the stronger meaning.

hot	slammed	exhausted
(boiling)	closed	tired
(crashed)	(gigantic)	hungry
fell	big	(starving)
cool	upset	looked
(icy)	(furious)	(stared)
(screamed)	damp	(pounded)
said	(soaked)	tapped

Page 94

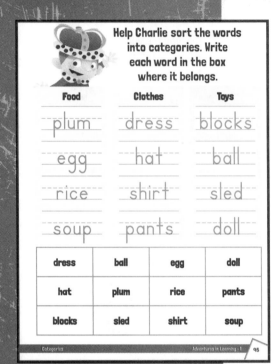

Help Charlie sort the words into categories. Write each word in the box where it belongs.

Food	Clothes	Toys
plum	dress	blocks
egg	hat	ball
rice	shirt	sled
soup	pants	doll

dress	ball	egg	doll
hat	plum	rice	pants
blocks	sled	shirt	soup

Page 95

Fill in the missing letters for each word.

shirt

pants

shoes

socks

shorts

dress

Page 96

Cut out the line of jewels.
Use the jewels to measure each object.

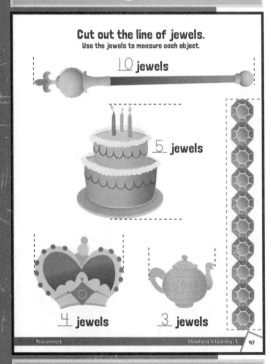

10 jewels

5 jewels

4 jewels

3 jewels

Page 97

ANSWER KEY

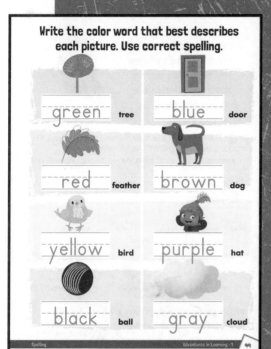

Write the color word that best describes each picture. Use correct spelling.

green tree
blue door
red feather
brown dog
yellow bird
purple hat
black ball
gray cloud

Page 99

Read each sentence. Draw a picture to show how Izzy or Charlie feels.

Izzy was nervous about the spelling test.

Drawings will vary.

Izzy was terrified about the troll at the door.

Charlie walked across the bridge.

Charlie raced across the bridge.

Page 100

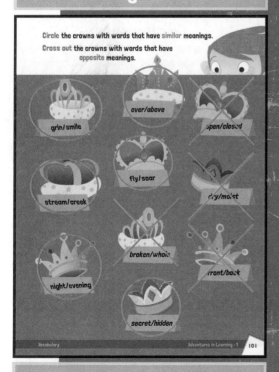

Circle the crowns with words that have similar meanings.
Cross out the crowns with words that have opposite meanings.

grin/smile
over/above
open/closed
fly/soar
stream/creek
dry/moist
night/evening
broken/whole
front/back
secret/hidden

Page 101

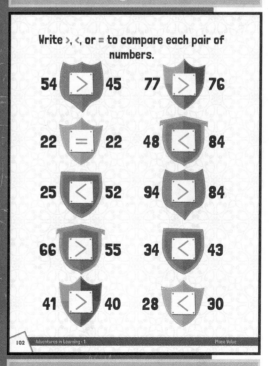

Write >, <, or = to compare each pair of numbers.

54 > 45   77 > 76
22 = 22   48 < 84
25 < 52   94 > 84
66 > 55   34 < 43
41 > 40   28 < 30

Page 102

ANSWER KEY

Page 103

Add or subtract each row. Then, add or subtract each column. Write the answers on the lines.

3	+	5	=	8
+		+		+
6	+	3	=	9
=		=		=
9	+	8	=	17

4	+	7	=	11
+		+		+
3	+	6	=	9
=		=		=
7	+	13	=	20

13	−	8	=	5
−		−		−
5	−	4	=	1
=		=		=
8	−	4	=	4

16	−	7	=	9
−		−		−
9	−	5	=	4
=		=		=
7	−	2	=	5

Addition, Subtraction   Adventures in Learning · 1   103

Page 104

Use context clues to make the best choice for each blue word's meaning. Circle your choice.

Izzy and Charlie invited all their friends to a huge feast. For dessert, they served 100 different cakes!
a sporting event   a long hike   (a big meal)

The way Daisy the dragon makes fire is fascinating to watch.
(very interesting)   very scary   very strange

Izzy tried to calm her horse after it was scared by a snake.
move   (quiet)   anger

Armor is worn to protect a knight during battle.
keep warm   (keep safe)   keep hidden

Charlie discovered an old painting in castle's basement.
opened   broke   (found)

104   Adventures in Learning · 1   Vocabulary

Page 106

Help Izzy solve the problems. Use the tens and ones blocks to add.

35
+ 8
43

23
+ 5
28

47
+ 2
49

53
+ 6
59

29
+ 3
32

106   Adventures in Learning · 1   Addition

Page 107

Verbs are words that tell what a person or a thing can do. Draw a line between the verbs below and the pictures that show action.

look

play

brush

read

grow

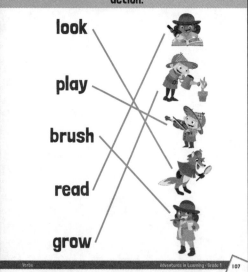

Verbs   Adventures in Learning · Grade 1   107

ANSWER KEY

Page 108

Look at the picture and read the words.
Write an **action word** in each sentence below.

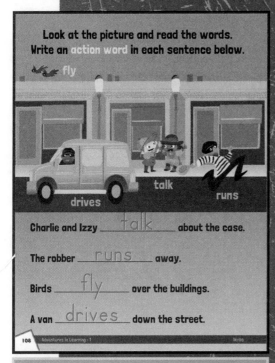

Charlie and Izzy ___talk___ about the case.

The robber ___runs___ away.

Birds ___fly___ over the buildings.

A van ___drives___ down the street.

Page 109

Help Charlie add.

17 + 2 19	20 + 5 25
18 + 4 22	36 + 3 39

24 + 7 31	32 + 7 39	14 + 8 22	41 + 6 47
29 + 8 37	34 + 6 40	27 + 4 31	31 + 9 40
19 + 4 23	33 + 9 42	51 + 4 55	49 + 7 56

Page 110

What time is it?
Write the time shown on each clock. One has been done as an example.

7:30

5:00

11:00

3:30

2:30

1:00

Page 111

Help Izzy and Charlie find the right verb.
Circle the verb that correctly completes the sentence.

The dog bark/(barks) when it sees a cat.

The plants (grow)/grows taller when
I water them.

Three balls (roll)/rolls down the hill.

Charlie look/(looks) for clues.

Izzy read/(reads) her notes.

They (solve)/solves the case.

The children (play)/plays soccer.

ANSWER KEY

When the subject of a sentence is singular, you use a singular verb. When the subject of a sentence is plural, you use a plural verb. Write a verb from the correct box to complete each sentence.

Singular Verbs
finds
chases
jumps

Plural Verbs
find
chase
jump

Charlie __finds__ a clue.

Izzy __chases__ a ball across the playground.

Charlie and Izzy __jump__ over a puddle.

They __chase__ a dog around the lake.

Charlie __jumps__ into the pool.

Charlie and Izzy __find__ a pretty rock.

Page 112

Count each set of objects. Write the number word to show how many.

__one__

__three__

__five__

__four__

__seven__

__two__

__six__

__nine__

Page 113

Help Charlie solve these problems.

There are 41 🏕 at Campground One.

There are 5 🏕 at Campground Two.

How many 🏕 in all?

__46__

One shelf has 18 ▪.

Another shelf has 6 ▪?

How many total ▪?

__24__

Charlie has 22 👓 in a box.

He has 9 more 👓 in another box.

How many 👓 in all?

__31__

Izzy saw 35 🔦 at the first store.

She saw 7 more 🔦 at the next store.

How many total 🔦 did Izzy see?

__42__

Page 114

Help Izzy organize.
Cut out each object below.
Then, sort them into two categories. Glue or tape each group into a closet.
Then, label each closet with the name of the category.

__wear__   __look through__

Page 115

ANSWER KEY

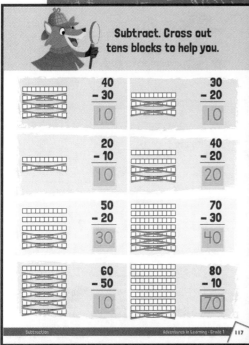

Subtract. Cross out tens blocks to help you.

40 − 30 = 10	30 − 20 = 10
20 − 10 = 10	40 − 20 = 20
50 − 20 = 30	70 − 30 = 40
60 − 50 = 10	80 − 10 = 70

Subtraction · Adventures in Learning · Grade 1 · 117

Page 117

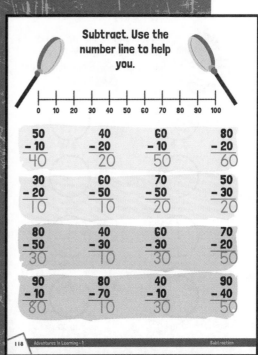

Subtract. Use the number line to help you.

0 10 20 30 40 50 60 70 80 90 100

50 − 10 = 40	40 − 20 = 20	60 − 10 = 50	80 − 20 = 60
30 − 20 = 10	60 − 50 = 10	70 − 50 = 20	50 − 30 = 20
80 − 50 = 30	40 − 30 = 10	60 − 30 = 30	70 − 20 = 50
90 − 10 = 80	80 − 70 = 10	40 − 10 = 30	90 − 40 = 50

118 · Adventures in Learning · 1 · Subtraction

Page 118

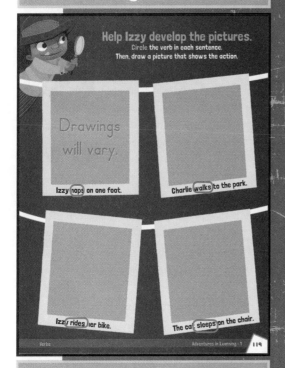

Help Izzy develop the pictures.
Circle the verb in each sentence.
Then, draw a picture that shows the action.

Drawings will vary.

Izzy (hops) on one foot.

Charlie (walks) to the park.

Izzy (rides) her bike.

The cat (sleeps) on the chair.

Verbs · Adventures in Learning · 1 · 119

Page 119

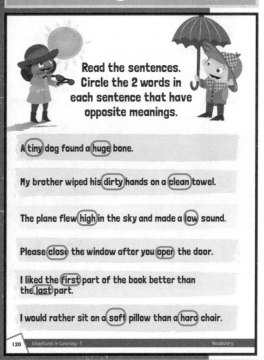

Read the sentences. Circle the 2 words in each sentence that have opposite meanings.

A (tiny) dog found a (huge) bone.

My brother wiped his (dirty) hands on a (clean) towel.

The plane flew (high) in the sky and made a (low) sound.

Please (close) the window after you (open) the door.

I liked the (first) part of the book better than the (last) part.

I would rather sit on a (soft) pillow than a (hard) chair.

120 · Adventures in Learning · 1 · Vocabulary

Page 120

ANSWER KEY

Someone stole the hands from these clocks! Draw hands on each clock to show the time.

7:00 9:30

1:30 4:30

12:00 4:00

3:30 10:00

Page 121

Help solve the case of the missing verbs! Write a verb to complete each sentence.

Answers will vary. Possible answers:

The frog _jumps_ .

The pig _oinks_ .

The fox _runs_ .

The fish _swims_ .

The duck _quacks_ .

The dog _barks_ .

Page 122

Match each shape to an object in the picture. Draw a line to connect them.

Page 123

Read the sentences. Circle the nouns. Draw a line under the verbs.

The (horse) runs fast.

The (car) drives by my (house).

(Charlie) plays with a (yo-yo).

The (squirrel) eats a (cookie).

(Izzy) looks for (clues).

Page 124

ANSWER KEY

Page 125

Help Izzy solve these problems.

There are 40 [markers] in a box.
Charlie takes 10 [markers] from the box. How many left in the box? **30**

The store has 70 [lemons] when it opens. The store sells 40 [lemons] during the day. How many are left at the end of the day? **30**

Pond A has 50 [frogs].
Pond B has 20 [frogs].
How many more [frogs] are in Pond A? **30**

There are 60 [spoons] in the drawer.
There are 50 [forks] in the drawer.
What is the difference? **10**

Charlie has 80¢.
Izzy has 30¢.
What is the difference? **50¢**

Page 126

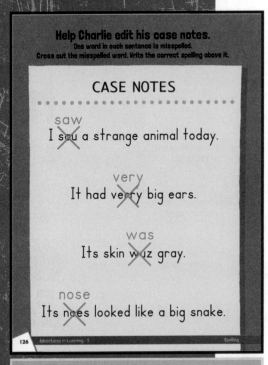

Help Charlie edit his case notes.
One word in each sentence is misspelled.
Cross out the misspelled word. Write the correct spelling above it.

CASE NOTES

saw
I ~~sau~~ a strange animal today.

very
It had ~~verry~~ big ears.

was
Its skin ~~wuz~~ gray.

nose
Its ~~noes~~ looked like a big snake.

Page 127

CASE NOTES

said
Izzy ~~sed~~ it was not strange.

me
She told ~~mee~~ it was an elephant.

zoo
We were at the ~~zew~~!

Page 128

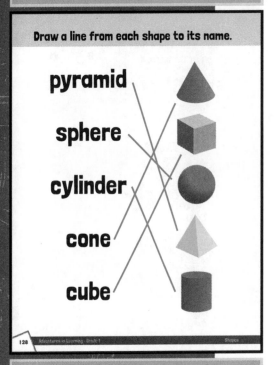

Draw a line from each shape to its name.

pyramid

sphere

cylinder

cone

cube

ANSWER KEY

Answers will vary. Possible answers:

Izzy saw a pretty horse. — brown

A green snake moved in the grass. — scary

Charlie ate a tasty ice cream cone. — cold

I picked a plump tomato from the garden. — red

There are big safes at the bank. — three

Page 129

Earn your Spelling Detective badge! Circle the misspelled word in each sentence. Write the correct spelling on the line.

Izzy has (too) pairs of glasses. — two

Charlie played checkers and (one) the game. — won

A book was stolen (frum) the library. — from

Izzy and Charlie (our) looking for clues. — are

(Wear) did you put the flashlight? — where

(Sum) people like to go fishing. — some

The puppy is only (for) days old. — four

Page 130

Write the numbers to show the time on each watch.

1:30   6:30

11:00   2:00

2:30   9:00

Page 131

Add or subtract

12	21	30	42
+ 5	+ 7	− 10	+ 7
17	28	20	49

80	45	22	18
− 20	+ 9	+ 8	− 9
60	54	30	9

80	45	70	90
+ 9	+ 6	− 30	− 40
89	51	40	50

20	39	25	57
− 8	+ 4	+ 8	+ 6
12	43	33	63

Page 132

ANSWER KEY

Page 133

Help Charlie and Izzy file their notes.

Cut out the words. Then, put each word into the correct file drawer.

noun: tub, clue, cup, pig, table
adjective: scary, wet, round, green, tall
verb: chase, draw, swim, jump, eat

Page 135

Label the shapes. Write C in all the circles. Write R in all the rectangles. Write T in all the triangles. Write S in all the squares.

C R S T R
R C C S T
S T S R C
T C T R S

Page 136

Use the objects to help you test the equations. Circle the equations that are true.

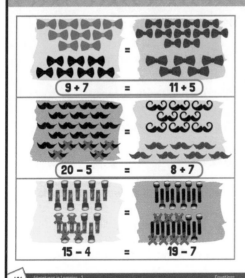

(9 + 7) = (11 + 5)

20 – 5 = 8 + 7

(15 – 4) = (19 – 7)

Page 137

Add an adjective to each sentence. Look at

Answers will vary. Possible answers:

Izzy made a __fun__ snowman.

A __big__ bus rumbled down the street.

I saw a __colorful__ rainbow after the storm.

We ate __hot__ soup for lunch.

__Two__ turtles walked to the pond.

ANSWER KEY

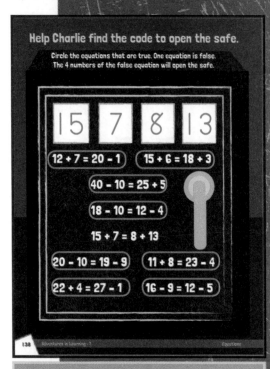

Page 138

Page 139

Page 140

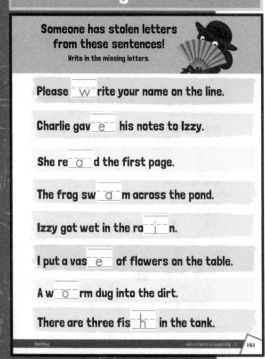

Page 141

ANSWER KEY

Rewrite each addition problem as a subtraction problem. The first one has been done as an example.

12 + 9 = 21	21 − 9 = 12
24 + 5 = 29	29 − 5 = 24
15 + 7 = 22	22 − 7 = 15
33 + 4 = 37	37 − 4 = 33
27 + 6 = 33	33 − 6 = 27
40 + 8 = 48	48 − 8 = 40
35 + 7 = 42	42 − 7 = 35
23 + 9 = 32	32 − 9 = 23
37 + 4 = 41	41 − 4 = 37
42 + 9 = 51	51 − 9 = 42

142   Adventures in Learning · 1   Addition, Subtraction

Page 142

Now, rewrite each subtraction problem as an addition problem. The first one has been done as an example.

22 − 8 = 14	14 + 8 = 22
27 − 5 = 22	22 + 5 = 27
21 − 7 = 14	14 + 7 = 21
30 − 6 = 24	24 + 6 = 30
33 − 4 = 29	29 + 4 = 33
41 − 5 = 36	36 + 5 = 41
35 − 9 = 26	26 + 9 = 35
19 − 9 = 10	10 + 9 = 19
27 − 8 = 19	19 + 8 = 27
32 − 5 = 27	27 + 5 = 32

Addition, Subtraction   Adventures in Learning · 1   143

Page 143

The letters in each word are mixed up. Write each word correctly.

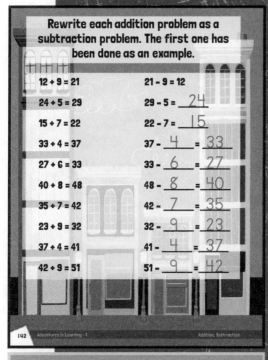

	onil	lion
	unbny	bunny
	kudc	duck
	agot	goat
	braze	zebra
	resho	horse

144   Adventures in Learning · 1   Spelling

Page 144

Help Charlie finish writing his case notes.

Add a prepositional phrase that answers the question *Where?*
The first one is done as an example.

CASE NOTES

I found a coin **under the desk**.

Possible answers:

Izzy parked her bike
by the door

My coat is hanging
in the closet

I hid the book
under a chair

Izzy put her camera
on the shelf

Sentences   Adventures in Learning · 1   145

Page 145

ANSWER KEY

Solve each equation.
Then, circle true or false.

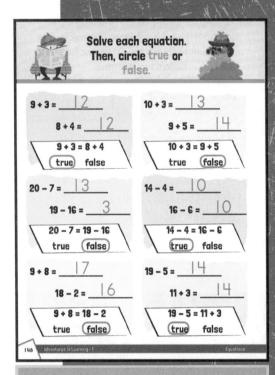

$9 + 3 = \underline{12}$

$8 + 4 = \underline{12}$

$9 + 3 = 8 + 4$
(true) false

$20 - 7 = \underline{13}$

$19 - 16 = \underline{3}$

$20 - 7 = 19 - 16$
true (false)

$9 + 8 = \underline{17}$

$18 - 2 = \underline{16}$

$9 + 8 = 18 - 2$
true (false)

$10 + 3 = \underline{13}$

$9 + 5 = \underline{14}$

$10 + 3 = 9 + 5$
true (false)

$14 - 4 = \underline{10}$

$16 - 6 = \underline{10}$

$14 - 4 = 16 - 6$
(true) false

$19 - 5 = \underline{14}$

$11 + 3 = \underline{14}$

$19 - 5 = 11 + 3$
(true) false

146 Adventures in Learning · 1   Equations

Page 146

Read each group of words. Place an X on the word that does not belong.

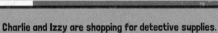

down, behind, wet (X), over, under

hawk, dove, parrot, rabbit (X), chicken

lion, hippo, tiger, monkey, tree (X)

dirt, rock, tree (X), water, sand

glasses (X), eyes, nose, ear, hair

Categories   Adventures in Learning · 1 147

Page 147

Charlie and Izzy are shopping for detective supplies.

Count the cameras in both cabinets. Then, write a number sentence to show the total number of cameras for sale.

$7 + 8 = 15$

148 Adventures in Learning · 1   Equations

Page 148

Count the magnifying glasses in both cabinets. Then, write a number sentence to show how many more are in the first cabinet.

$14 - 5 = 9$

Equations   Adventures in Learning · 1 149

Page 149

ANSWER KEY

Page 150

Read each sentence. Draw a picture to show how Izzy or Charlie feels.

Izzy enjoyed the cool breeze.	Izzy shivered in the icy breeze.
Drawings will vary.	
Charlie walked a small dog.	Charlie walked a tiny dog.

150 Adventures in Learning · 1   Vocabulary

Page 151

Expand each sentence by adding a word that ___ in

Answers will vary. Possible answers:

Charlie wore a ___nice___ hat. (What kind?)

___Two___ dogs played at the park. (How many?)

Izzy's ___old___ coat is hanging in the closet. (Which one?)

The ___sneaky___ fox hid behind the door. (Which one?)

I gave Izzy ___three___ keys that I found. (How many?)

A ___fast___ car sped around the corner. (What kind?)

The ___pretty___ bird landed on top of a mailbox. (Which one?)

Charlie broke his ___new___ pair of sunglasses. (What kind?)

___Four___ children ran across the bridge. (How many?)

Sentences   Adventures in Learning · 1 151

Page 152

Some words sound the same, but they have different spellings and meanings.

Help Izzy choose the right word. Circle the word that correctly completes each sentence.

CASE NOTES

___ is Charlie going?
Wear (Where)

I think he is walking ___ the store.
(to) too

I wonder what he will ___ there?
by (buy)

I hope it is a treat ___ me!
four (for)

152 Adventures in Learning · 1   Spelling

Page 153

Cut out the shapes at the bottom of the page. Then, tape or glue each shape into the box that names it.

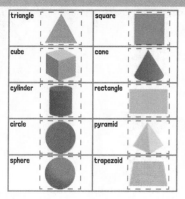

triangle	square
cube	cone
cylinder	rectangle
circle	pyramid
sphere	trapezoid

Shapes   Adventures in Learning · 1 153

ANSWER KEY

Page 156

Match the monsters.
Find 3 monsters that look alike.
Use the numbers on the 3 matching monsters to write a math problem.
You will need to write 2 addition problems and 2 subtractions problems.

$\underline{3} + \underline{5} = \underline{8}$ Answers will vary. Possible answers: $\underline{15} - \underline{7} = \underline{8}$

$\underline{4} + \underline{8} = \underline{12}$ $\underline{13} - \underline{9} = \underline{4}$

156   Adventures in Learning · 1   Equations

Page 157

Circle the sentences that tell about the past.

(The monster cried.)   The monster cries.

(The monster waved.)   The monster waves.

The monsters smile.   (The monsters smiled.)

The monster dances.   (The monster danced.)

The monster runs.   (The monster ran.)

Verbs   Adventures in Learning · 1   157

Page 158

Help the monsters move in.

Read each word.
Write the words in the rooms where you think they go.

TV	dishes	clothes
couch	pans	pillow
dresser	books	fruit
mirror	computer	forks

158   Adventures in Learning · 1   Categories

Page 159

The monster thinks all of his answers are correct.
Check his work to see. If an answer is wrong, cross it out. Then, write the correct answer.

12	40	46
+ 8	− 20	+ 5
20	20	51

62	80	27
+ 7	− 20	+ 4
~~70~~ 69	60	31

55	24	70
+ 2	+ 8	− 40
57	32	~~20~~ 30

38	41	43
+ 5	+ 9	+ 6
43	50	~~44~~ 49

Addition, Subtraction   Adventures in Learning · 1   159

ANSWER KEY

Many present-tense verbs are changed to past tense by adding –ed. Add –ed to the following verbs to make them past tense.

climb **ed**
wash **ed**
play **ed**
open **ed**   watch **ed**
help **ed**   clean **ed**
look **ed**   talk **ed**

If the present-tense verb already ends with –e, then just add –d. Add –d to the following verbs to make them past tense.

rake **d**   close **d**   hike **d**
bake **d**   chase **d**   care **d**
hope **d**   save **d**   share **d**

Page 160

Read the times. Draw the hands and write the numbers for each given time.

five thirty
5:30

three o'clock
3:00

nine thirty
9:30

Page 161

The monsters are visiting the city. They see lots of signs, but they see lots of mistakes, too.

Circle the misspelled words. Write the correct spellings on the lines below.

TOODAY'S SPECIAL: Dog Food ½ price

BY SOME TODAY!

Save BIG at BIG Bob's!

Candee Shop

today's
buy
candy

Page 162

Frank's Cheese Stoer

Toys Four Sale Inside!

HELP WONTED

Music Shop

store
for
wanted

Page 163

ANSWER KEY

Page 164

Look at each figure. Decide if the monster can roll it, stack it, or do both.
Circle the answer(s).

(roll) (stack)

roll (stack)

(roll) stack

Page 165

roll (stack)

roll (stack)

(roll) stack

Page 166

Use a ^ to add the phrase in parentheses to the sentence. The first one is done as an example.

to the park
Izzy walked ^ yesterday.   (to the park)

from the jar
The monster took a cookie.^   (from the jar)

in the vase
The flowers ^ are for Mom.   (in the vase)

up the driveway
Charlie rode his bike.^   (up the driveway)

on the chair
The cat is asleep.^   (on the chair)

with three eyes
The monster ^ is jumping.   (with three eyes)

Page 167

Circle the past-tense verb on each kite.

ANSWER KEY

Page 168

Fill in the missing number to complete each equation.

$$\begin{array}{r} 8 \\ + \boxed{7} \\ \hline 15 \end{array} \qquad \begin{array}{r} \boxed{9} \\ + 6 \\ \hline 15 \end{array} \qquad \begin{array}{r} 12 \\ + \boxed{7} \\ \hline 19 \end{array}$$

$$\begin{array}{r} \boxed{8} \\ + 5 \\ \hline 13 \end{array} \qquad \begin{array}{r} 15 \\ + \boxed{5} \\ \hline 20 \end{array} \qquad \begin{array}{r} 11 \\ + 7 \\ \hline 18 \end{array}$$

$$13 + \boxed{7} = 20$$

$$\boxed{10} + 10 = 20$$

168 Adventures in Learning · 1   Equations

Page 169

Circle the word that best completes each sentence.

A strong breeze closed/**slammed** the door shut.

After the race, the runners quickly **gulped**/sipped cups of water.

Izzy felt **great**/okay about winning the writing contest.

The team scored, and the crowd **screamed**/said, "Hooray!"

My clothes were damp/**soaked** when I got caught in the heavy downpour.

Vocabulary   Adventures in Learning · 1 169

Page 170

Write the color name for each monster. Cross out letters in the box as you use them. The letters that are left will spell one more color. Write the color, and draw a monster to match it.

l r g r l u n d e w
l e e p e y p r o e

purple   blue

yellow   red

170 Adventures in Learning · 1   Spelling

Page 171

Welcome to the Monster Museum of Art.
Cut out the titles below.
Glue or tape each title next to the artwork it describes.

No Angles

Three Angles

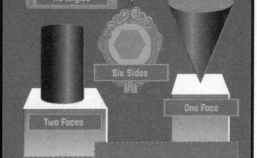

Six Sides

Two Faces

One Face

Shapes   Adventures in Learning · 1 171

ANSWER KEY

Page 173

Sometimes sentences have 2 verbs. Circle the verbs in each sentence.

The monster (smiled) and (waved) his arms.

The monster (saw) a bird and (pointed) at it.

The monster (climbed) into his bed and slept.

The monster (made) a sandwich and (ate) it.

Izzy (ran) and (played) at the park.

Page 174

Use context clues to make the best choice for each red word's meaning.
Circle your choice.

The monsters were ecstatic about the new swimming pool. They smiled and roared, "New pool!" Then, they jumped in and played.
empty (happy) pretty

One monster fell down in the yard during lunch. She hurt her arm. The ache got worse when she tried to swim again.
dream   water   (pain)

Please listen now. I don't want to have to repeat this later.
(say again)   think about   leave

Page 175

The monsters' clocks are all wrong. Each clock is a half hour slow. Draw hands on the blank clocks to show a half hour later. The first one has been done for you.

Page 176

Write the correct present- or past-tense verb in the blank.

Last year, the monster _cried_ when it was time to take a bath.
cries   cried

Now, the monster _loves_ taking baths.
loved   loves

He _feels_ clean and fresh whenever he takes a bath.
felt   feels

After his bath last night, the monster _smelled_ great.
smells   smelled

The monster always _giggles_ when he scrubs his toes.
giggles   giggled

ANSWER KEY

Page 177

Help the monster spot the mistakes. Circle the misspelled word in each set. Then, write the correct spelling.

man	(boi)	woman	boy
doctor	(chiled)	teacher	child
fish	frog	(gote)	goat
(shurt)	dress	shoes	shirt
(three)	four	five	three
green	(bloo)	yellow	blue
lion	(hors)	monkey	horse
(chiar)	lamp	couch	chair

Spelling   Adventures in Learning · 1   177

Page 178

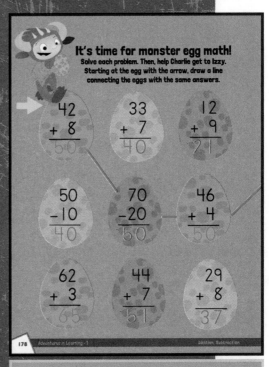

It's time for monster egg math! Solve each problem. Then, help Charlie get to Izzy. Starting at the egg with the arrow, draw a line connecting the eggs with the same answers.

$$42 + 8 = 50$$ $$33 + 7 = 40$$ $$12 + 9 = 21$$

$$50 - 10 = 40$$ $$70 - 20 = 50$$ $$46 + 4 = 50$$

$$62 + 3 = 65$$ $$44 + 7 = 51$$ $$29 + 8 = 37$$

178   Adventures in Learning · 1   Addition, Subtraction

Page 179

$$14 + 9 = 23$$ $$60 - 20 = 40$$ $$38 - 2 = 36$$

$$55 - 5 = 50$$ $$27 + 5 = 32$$ $$36 + 8 = 44$$

$$70 - 30 = 40$$ $$41 + 9 = 50$$ $$90 - 40 = 50$$

Addition, Subtraction   Adventures in Learning · 1   179

Page 180

Write each verb in the correct column.

slept   smiles   sang   take   found
hid   sees   plays   flew   carry

Yesterday	Today
slept	smiles
hid	sees
sang	plays
flew	take
found	carry

180   Adventures in Learning · 1   Verbs

ANSWER KEY

Page 181

Expand each sentence by writing a second verb on the line.

Izzy dances and __plays__ for her friends.

Please close the door and __sit__.

The ball bounces and __rolls__.

The cup fell off the table and __broke__.

Charlie played and __ran__ at the park.

The ice cracks and __melts__ in spring.

I turn off the light and __sleeps__.

Sentences · Adventures in Learning · 1 · 181

Page 181

Page 182

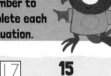

Fill in the missing number to complete each equation.

$$19 - \boxed{7} = 12$$

$$\boxed{17} - 4 = 13$$

$$15 - \boxed{8} = 7$$

$$\boxed{19} - 9 = 10$$

$$13 - \boxed{8} = 5$$

$$\boxed{20} - 18 = 2$$

$$17 - \boxed{10} = 7 \qquad \boxed{19} - 8 = 11$$

182 · Adventures in Learning · 1 · Equations

Page 182

Page 183

Help the monsters add commas (,).

Commas separate the items in a list in a sentence.
Add a comma below each monster.
One has been done for you.

I like to have eggs, toast, and juice for breakfast.

Reading, soccer, and drawing are my hobbies.

We went to the store, the library, and the park today.

Sentences · Adventures in Learning · 1 · 183

Page 183

Page 184

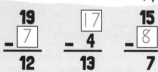

Solve each equation. Use the tens blocks for help. Then, circle True or False.

$$40 + 40 = \underline{80}$$

$$80 - 30 = \underline{50}$$

$$20 + 50 = \underline{70}$$

$$90 - 40 = \underline{50}$$

40 + 40 = 20 + 50
true (false)

80 - 30 = 90 - 40
(true) false

184 · Adventures in Learning · Grade 1 · Equations

Page 184

ANSWER KEY

Page 185

How many eyes in all? Write the equation shown by the 10-eyed monsters and the 1-eyed monsters.

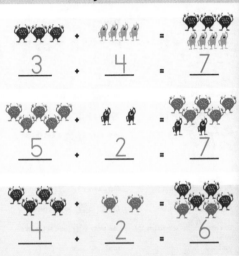

$$3 + 4 = 7$$

$$5 + 2 = 7$$

$$4 + 2 = 6$$

Equations   Adventures in Learning · 1   185

Page 186

Use context clues to make the best choice for each yellow word's meaning.
Circle your choice.

The monsters hoped there would be no precipitation today, but it stormed anyway, and they all got wet.

a bad day   (rain or snow)   umbrellas

Please speak up. I can't hear you when you mumble.

(talk quietly)   eat   walk away

Would you prefer to wear the pink shirt or the striped shirt?

clean   put away   (like better)

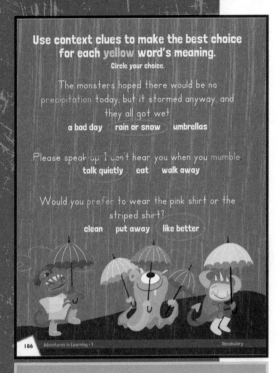

186   Adventures in Learning · 1   Vocabulary

Page 187

Help the monster find the right shapes. Color the shape that fits each description.

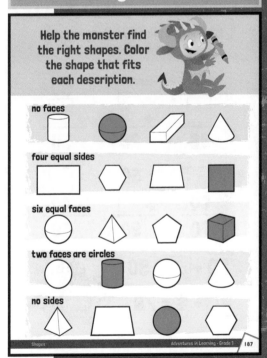

no faces

four equal sides

six equal faces

two faces are circles

no sides

Shapes   Adventures in Learning · Grade 1   187

Page 188

When you add the helping verb will, you tell about what will happen later.

Add the helping verb will to complete each future tense verb.

Tomorrow, the monster __will__ drive to the beach.

He __will__ swim in the ocean.

He __will__ play in the sand.

188   Adventures in Learning · 1   Verbs

ANSWER KEY

Write 2 sentences telling about something you will do in the future. Then, draw a picture of what you will do.

Answers and drawings will vary.

I will _____ .

I will _____ .

Page 189

Solve.

There are 53 . There are 47 .
There are 7 . There are 8 .
How many and total? How many and total?
60 **55**

There were 70 . 60 came to a party.
The monsters ate 40 . 30 more came to the party.
How many are left? How many are at the party now?
30 **90**

50 rode on a bus. There were 80 at the park.
40 got off the bus. Then 60 left the park.
how many are still on the bus? How many are at the park now?
10 **20**

Page 190

Cut out the sentence parts. Then, match a part from the left to a part from the right to make compound sentences.

The monster was hungry, | so he ate a sandwich.
Charlie loves his new hat, | but Izzy thinks it looks silly.
I met a monster named Gordon, | and he was very friendly.
I saw a gift with my name on it, | but it was not my birthday.
The monster read a book, | and then he went to sleep.

Page 191

Fill in the missing number to complete each equation.

$$\begin{array}{r} 30 \\ + \boxed{8} \\ \hline 38 \end{array} \qquad \begin{array}{r} \boxed{20} \\ + 9 \\ \hline 29 \end{array} \qquad \begin{array}{r} 50 \\ + \boxed{5} \\ \hline 55 \end{array}$$

$$\begin{array}{r} \boxed{10} \\ + 60 \\ \hline 70 \end{array} \qquad \begin{array}{r} 50 \\ + \boxed{40} \\ \hline 90 \end{array} \qquad \begin{array}{r} \boxed{40} \\ + 40 \\ \hline 80 \end{array}$$

$$20 + \boxed{70} = 90$$

$$\boxed{70} + 8 = 78$$

Page 193

ANSWER KEY

The monster left his house at 1:00 to run errands.

On the lines, write the times when he got to each place.

bank	5 : 30
grocery store	2 : 30
post office	2 : 00
park	3 : 00

How long did it take to go from home to the park? 2 hours

Page 194

Add a verb to tell about each picture. Use the tense shown in parentheses ( ).

Answers will vary. Possible answers:

Izzy __hid__ from Charlie.
(past)

 Charlie __sits__ in a chair.
(present)

The monster __will have__ cake on his birthday.
(future)

 The fish __swims__ in the pond.
(present)

Charlie __walked__ to the store.
(past)

The monster __will jump__ rope at the park.
(future)

Page 195

Add commas to the sentences below.

The monster has a dog, a cat, and a bird as pets.

Lila, Sam, and Henry played a game.

I got a shirt, a jacket, and a pair of shoes at the store.

Mom, Dad, and Uncle Luis are planting flowers.

Maya put a cup, bowl, and spoon into the dishwasher.

The monster used paper, scissors, and paint to make a card.

Page 196

Fill in the missing number to complete each equation.

$$90 - \boxed{40} = 50$$
$$\boxed{50} - 40 = 10$$
$$80 - \boxed{25} = 55$$

$$\boxed{50} - 30 = 20$$
$$90 - \boxed{60} = 30$$
$$\boxed{90} - 30 = 60$$

$$80 - \boxed{20} = 60$$
$$\boxed{50} - 0 = 50$$

Page 197

ANSWER KEY

Write **3** sentences to tell about the picture.

Sentences will vary.

Page 198

Help the monsters hunt for 3–D shapes. Find objects around you that match each shape. Draw a picture of what you find.

Drawings will vary.

Page 199

Commas are used in dates to separate the month and day from the year. Commas also separate the day of the week from the month and day. Add commas to the sentences below. The first 2 have been done as examples.

School starts on August 21 , 2017.

The play is on Friday , March 3.

My book is due Thursday, May 13.

The monster was born June 20, 2012.

What holiday is on July 4, 2018?

My party is planned for Tuesday, September 12.

Ruby missed school on February 15, 2017.

We leave on Sunday, October 9.

Page 200

Help Izzy solve these problems.
Write an equation for each problem. Then, solve.

You have 64 pennies.
You find 9 more.
How many pennies do you have total?

$$64 + 9 = 73$$

A parking lot has 76 cars.
7 more cars park.
How many cars are in the lot now?

$$76 + 7 = 83$$

A shop has 70 apples.
30 apples are sold.
How many apples are left?

$$70 - 30 = 40$$

90 birds land in a tree.
Then 50 birds fly away.
How many birds are left?

$$90 - 50 = 40$$

Page 201

ANSWER KEY

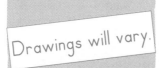

Tell the monster a bedtime math story! Think of a story problem for each equation. Draw a picture for the story. Then, fill in the missing number.

$$\begin{array}{r} 8 \\ + \boxed{9} \\ \hline 17 \end{array}$$

Drawings will vary.

$$\begin{array}{r} 14 \\ - \boxed{5} \\ \hline 9 \end{array}$$

202 Adventures in Learning · Grade 1 — Equations

Page 202

Circle the mistake in each sentence. Then, rewrite the sentence correctly.

There is a bike a scooter, and a ball in the shed.

There is a bike, a scooter, and a ball in the shed.

The monsters goes to the museum tomorrow.

The monsters go to the museum tomorrow.

Izzy sau a bird in the tree.

Izzy saw a bird in the tree.

Sentences — Adventures in Learning · Grade 1 — 203

Page 203

Write a word from the signs to answer each question. Use each word once.

sphere   cone   cube

pyramid   rectangular prism   cylinder

Which shape has four triangles for faces? __pyramid__

Which shape has a circle for its two faces? __cylinder__

Which shape has one circular face and one vertex (or "point")? __cone__

Which shape has six faces that are rectangles? __rectangular prism__

Which shape has six equal faces? __cube__

Which shape has no faces at all? __sphere__

204 Adventures in Learning · 1 — Shapes

Page 204

Answer Key   Adventures in Learning · Grade 1   251

Draw your own pirate ship.

Draw a prince and a princess on the towers.

Draw a detective by the fireplace.